2⁰⁰

DANCIN' TOWARD THE DAWN

"It has been my pleasure to use You Gotta' Keep Dancin' *and* Dancin' Toward the Dawn *at Loma Linda University Medical Center Rehabilitation Institute and Center for Pain Management. Our patients need to hear the story of Tim's struggles with chronic pain and how God can infuse joy into life amidst the suffering."*
Keith L. Dreiberg, Ph.D., M.P.H.,
Clinical Neuropsychologist

"Some people look loneliness in the eye and quake. Not Tim Hansel. Many times during his life, Tim has faced loneliness and all its side effects and overcome them with joy. His faith and trust in his Lord Jesus allows him to keep his eyes on his ultimate future. A prime example for all of us. You too can overcome loneliness."
Edward W. Bent,
Retired California State
Fire Service Training Supervisor

DANCIN'
TOWARD
THE DAWN

Discovering joy in the darkness of loneliness

TIM HANSEL

Cook Communications

Victor is an imprint of
Cook Communications Ministries, Colorado Springs, Colorado 80918
Cook Communications, Paris, Ontario
Kingsway communications, Eastbourne, England

DANCIN' TOWARD THE DAWN
© 1991, 2000 by Tim Hansel

Cover Design: Image Studios

Unless otherwise noted, all Scripture references are from the *Holy Bible, New International Version*®. Copyright © 1973, 1978, 1984 by International Bible Society. Used by permission of Zondervan Publishing House. All rights reserved; other references are from the *Authorized (King James) Version* (KJV); the *New American Standard Bible* (NASB), © the Lockman Foundation 1960, 1962, 1963, 1968, 1971, 1972, 1973, 1975, 1977; *The Living Bible* (TLB), © 1971 Tyndale House Publishers, Wheaton, IL 60189. Used by permission; *The New Testament in Modern English*, Revised Edition (Phillips), © J.B. Phillips, 1958, 1960, 1972, permission of Macmillan Publishing Co. and Collins Publishers.

First printing new edition, 2000
Printed in the United States of America

1 2 3 4 5 6 7 8 9 10 Printing/Year 04 03 02 01 00

Originally published as *Through the Wilderness of Loneliness*

Library of Congress Cataloging-in-Publication Data

Hansel, Tim.
   [Through the wilderness of loneliness]
   Dancin' toward the dawn: discovering joy in the darkness of loneliness /
     Tim Hansel. p. cm.
   Originally published: Through the wilderness of loneliness. Elgin, Ill. :
     D.C.Cook, c1991. With new introd.
   Includes bibliographical references.
   ISBN 1-56476-761-2
   1. Loneliness--Religious aspects--Christianity. 2. Christian life. I. Title:
   Dancing toward the dawn. II. Title.

BV4911 .H36 2000
248.8'6--dc21
                                         99-0555

DEDICATION

Eugene Kennedy reminds us that "friendship creates
the world in which we can comfortably be ourselves,
in which we are valued above all for that."

A friend is someone who understands your past,
believes in your future, and accepts you today anyway,
just the way you are.

To Chris Slagle
—Friend—
With whom I can be myself

A WORD FROM TIM HANSEL

As I SAT HERE STARING at the title and subtitle of this book, I thought, WOW! What a paradigm shift! That we actually can dance toward a *new* dawn in our lives. And even discover joy amidst the painful darkness of loneliness. It does sound a little outrageous, doesn't it? But the BEST PART is that it's ACTUALLY TRUE. In and through the living Christ He can and will help us discover a deeper joy than we ever dreamed possible *because loneliness does indeed parch our lips for a deeper experience of Him, and others, even of understanding and learning how to truly love ourselves properly (as He loves us no more, but certainly not less either).*

Jesus stands unchallenged as the greatest paradigm buster of all time. It still surprises me that people don't gasp more when they read Scripture—or get red faced with either exasperation or joy, or do cartwheels. So I hope that when you read a title like *Dancin' Toward the Dawn* at least your blood pressure changes or the bell on your pacemaker goes off!

I'm humbled and almost overwhelmed by the impact that this book has made on so many people's lives. Counselors have told me that they recommend it to all their clients. I've continued to receive letters and calls from people all over the country letting me know *Dancin' Toward the Dawn* has transformed their lives. These responses have not only encouraged me to keep on writing, but most of all have reminded me again that God can use anybody and any means of communication as His vehicle to change a life.

I pray that God will use this book to touch your life too.

Tim Hansel
Seattle
September 1999

ABOUT THE AUTHOR

Meet TIM HANSEL: author, speaker, mountain climber. Storyteller and encourager. Husband, dad, and grandfather. Fellow struggler in God's great family.

In 1974, Tim suffered a climbing accident that should have left him paralyzed . . . if not dead. Instead, he climbed back out of the six-stories-deep crevasse into which he had fallen, upside down, and the next day hiked 22 miles out to his car and drove himself over 350 miles home!—evidence of God's amazing strength and grace. Throughout the intervening years, Tim has continued to deal with chronic pain and its companion problems. The pain has cost him not only his physical health, but emotional stress, broken relationships—including a divorce, and endurance of spiritual wildernesses as well. Learning to find joy within the pain was the theme of *You Gotta' Keep Dancin'*, which has sold over 225,000 copies since 1985.

Although Tim was declared permanently disabled in 1988 he has continued to reach out to fellow sufferers in many ways through his ministry *ignite!*, which strives to "motivate, encourage, and empower people," speaking, teaching, writing, and one-on-one as people seek him out for counsel and encouragement. He and his wife, Anastasia, have dedicated themselves to a life of compassion, coming alongside those that most of society has little time for.

In *Dancin' Toward the Dawn*, Tim offers his inimitable blend of humor, personal experience, Scripture, and inspirational anecdotes, liberally salted with his favorite quotations from a diverse parade of authors. His goal is to encourage anyone who has ever known the pain of loneliness . . . and that includes all of us. Let Tim be your guide, and discover what God has in store for you. As someone recently told him following a speaking engagement, "God has given you a way of making the heavy bearable, the holy accessible, and the consistent possible."

To find out more about ignite! *or for information regarding films, books, or speaking engagements, write to:*

Tim and Anastasia Hansel
910 19th Avenue East
Seattle, WA 98112

or call:
206-323-0247

The proceeds from Dancin' Toward the Dawn *will go to* ignite! *to touch the hearts of people.*

TABLE OF CONTENTS

Why the Wilderness?

We need the tonic of the wilderness.
—HENRY DAVID THOREAU

*Life is God's great classroom; the
wilderness is God's great place of training.*
—JIM WILSON

FOR THE PAST TWENTY YEARS, I've been involved in a wilderness school for people of all ages. We've had participants as young as six and as old as seventy-four. We've had people weighing less than eighty pounds and some who tipped in at over three hundred pounds. Summit has run courses for the physically disabled and courses for members of the United Nations. We are now convinced that virtually anyone can enjoy the wilderness experience.

In the wilderness you experience life firsthand. If you don't fix dinner, you don't eat. If you don't help everyone across the river, you don't get to the other side. If you don't put up the shelter, you get wet. There is no avoiding simple consequences. There is no avoiding life. Without any props, without any distractions, people grow because they have to.

Throughout the past two decades in the wilderness, I've seen that wilderness experiences are very biblical. Abraham had a wilderness experience. So did Moses. Joshua, David, and Elijah knew what the wilderness was all about. Jesus had more than one wilderness experience. So did the apostle Paul.

Like the Israelites at the time of the Exodus, in the wilderness we are stripped of our normal conveniences and asked to make a journey into the unknown. The wilderness—whether exterior or interior—is always a time of radical dependence upon God. It is often a time of great difficulty; when the going got tough for God's chosen people, they often complained that they would rather be back under the control of the Egyptians so they could have some of their conveniences back. But their wilderness experience was never intended to be an end in itself; it was a time of preparation for a promise. And the wilderness is a place of great adventure.

> *That's where faith begins . . . in the wilderness, when you are all alone and afraid, when things don't make any sense.*
> —ELISABETH ELLIOT

HAVING SPENT SO MUCH time in the wilderness of mountains and desert, I can see that the wilderness is a marvelous metaphor for our inner journey . . . our spiritual pilgrimage . . . our "journey of the heart." In many ways, the interior wilderness is infinitely more difficult and complex.

In Scripture a wilderness experience always has a distinct purpose and it always leads to a promise. The same is true of the interior wilderness; it is likewise a time of radical dependence, of training for a purpose and, if we go through it, it will also lead to a promise. It has a gift hidden within.

The Bible is a wilderness book. It talks a lot about faith. And faith is always a leap into the uncharted. You can't tiptoe across a chasm, nor can you take it in two leaps. Faith is the ultimate gamble. It takes immense courage.

The wilderness is unknown. It is unpredictable. We go into our interior wilderness in order to learn, to discover, to grow. We never know what will happen. We're boldly asking God to surprise us, overwhelm us, stun us again with His presence and His love.

> *I went to the woods because I wanted to*
> *see if I could not learn what life had to*
> *teach—and not, when I came to die,*
> *discover that I had not lived.*
> —HENRY DAVID THOREAU

I WAS ONCE ASKED TO SPEAK at the Pacific Palisades Presbyterian Conference Center to a group of men. We arrived at the camp at a little after five. It was a rustic place, nestled in the woods up against a national forest and inviting mountains. I was stiff and in a lot of pain, so I decided to go for a walk. I wasn't more than a hundred yards up the trail when my whole being began to shout: "I love the wilderness!" I like exploring new trails, sniffing new scents, seeing new terrain.

The trail was rugged and steep in places. My body began to sweat, and I began to release some of those God-given endorphins. The pain moved over to make room for beauty and newness. I felt uniquely alive again. I walked up until I knew the darkness was setting in. As I came back down it was quickly getting darker, and my senses came alive in even more extraordinary ways. I listened more intently to every sound. My eyes adjusted so I could see in the fading light. I felt my muscles much more intensely. I had a kinetic focus now like a sharp beam of light.

I realized that I like the darkness. I didn't need to avoid it; I didn't have to hurry or run. I could see the light where the camp was, and I could feel my way back.

So, too, with the dark times of our soul. These times give us a new opportunity to explore our feelings. If only we are not afraid to relax in the present and become more aware, there is enough light to walk in the darkness of the wilderness.

I have found that I can even enjoy the inner wilderness. Feeling new feelings, taking a chance, not playing it safe, getting in touch with more of me. I don't need to avoid the painful experiences in my life. It requires going behind the words to the music, even if it is a little off-key. It means experiencing my feelings fully. Experiencing God. Making real contact. Letting my heart be thrashed and rearranged if necessary.

The wilderness of the heart is a place where life happens!

There is no shortcut to wholeness: if you want to reach the Promised Land you must first go through the wilderness.
—CLIFTON BURKE

W HEN IT COMES to the wilderness of the heart, we must likewise expect the unexpected. The dark feelings have something to teach me which I can learn no other way. I must open up to all that God wants to teach me. There are experiences that He wants to give me so I can learn. Nobody else can experience it for me, nor can I experience it if I keep pushing it away by distraction and detour.

The only way out is through. It takes courage, tenacity,

stamina, patience, God's immense grace, and time. If God is going to make His imprint in our lives, we must be willing to go through our feelings—not to let them dictate to us, but just to experience them. Detours and distractions always end up as dead ends. Emotions are what give relationships their essence. They help us know where we are. There is no such thing as an up without a down, a back without a front, a left without a right, an inside without an outside. We need to experience the whole spectrum.

Experience is a different teacher, giving you the test first and the lessons after.

—ANONYMOUS

When God is going to do something wonderful, He begins with a difficulty. If He is going to do something very wonderful, He begins with an impossibility.

—DEWEY CASS

A MAP IS NOT THE SAME as being there. A map shows you where to go and how to get there. It shows you where the high places are and what they will be like. But it is no substitute for the wilderness itself.

The Bible is a map and a survival manual for the Christian life. The Holy Spirit is the compass and our personal guide. But we still have to put our boots on and explore the wilderness ourselves. We can't get there by taxi.

None of us knows exactly what we will find. There will be difficult places as well as awesome beauty. There will be hard grinds and oases. There will be moving experiences, and some experiences we would like to avoid altogether.

But the more time we spend in the wilderness, the more comfortable we become there. The rugged terrain turns into veritable adventure. The unique beauty is an invitation to the mystery of living, and we begin to appreciate the gift of each day.

The Pain of Loneliness

*Like it or not, we are as vulnerable to
loneliness as we are to the common cold.*
—BEN FERGUSON

*The pain of loneliness is one way in which
[God] gets our attention.*
—ELISABETH ELLIOT

LONELINESS IS a wrinkled and unappreciated feeling . . .
like a well-worn pair of faded jeans. It's the kind of feeling you find
in the corner of the closet when you're not even looking for it. A
leftover ache, rumpled in the corner—which somehow manages to
penetrate your whole being.

I have thought at times that there is no pain quite so empty as
loneliness. It is the pain of simply being alive. We've all tasted it.
There is no life without relationships—and there can be no relationships without loneliness. Loneliness and love are inseparable twins.

Our hearts are ragged and scarred with our attempts to love and be loved, and sometimes with the pain of finding love.

Loneliness may be one of the most difficult experiences that any of us will have to face. It's that inner vacuum that nothing seems to be able to fill. A void. An emptiness. An ache that nothing is able to fix. A pain that is elusive, evasive, and hard to handle.

Sometimes there's nothing quite as desperate as feeling all alone. Trapped in your own isolation, it feels like you are in a house with all the windows blackened out so that there is no sunlight coming through. There is an inner darkness that can't seem to be pushed out; however, there's a great truth that "when you can't push the darkness out, you can let the light in." We may be lonely, but we are not alone.

In this book we will explore the wilderness of loneliness and discover how to let the light in. For it is my premise that loneliness can be a unique gift from God—a vehicle through which we get to know Him better. Loneliness is like a caterpillar in a cocoon. It feels lonely and isolated, but it is God's way of preparing to give us new wings of freedom. As we journey from loneliness to love, we do it through the tunnel of solitude—where we again discover that God loves us truly and fully for who we are and not who we think we should be.

*The pressures and problems of our
complex society have produced a world of
lonely people jammed together like
sardines in a can we call "earth."*
—CARL JUNG

*FROM MY JOURNAL:
The loneliness was so bad tonight that it
sucked all the oxygen out of the room. It
was so intense it felt like it could peel the
paint off the walls.*

THEY LAUGHED RICHLY last night. The building
vibrated with joy. "I haven't had so much fun in years." "You are
the best speaker I've ever heard." "Please come again."

And then, when it was all over, the books signed and the hands
shaken, I drove back to my hotel. I had intentionally left the lights
on in my room so it wouldn't seem so dark and lonely when I came
back in.

All hotel rooms aren't really the same; they just feel that way.
The emptiness resounds off the mandatory chair, table, Formica
top, and imitation paintings.

I sit down on the bed. My starched shirt is wrinkled, and so is
my heart. The pain that I blocked out while speaking comes back

to amplify my loneliness. I can't sleep because of the pain and because I'm in a different time zone. I'm too tired to read, and the TV seems like mere noisy din on the inside of a large cardboard crate. So I wander around the corridors of my heart until I realize that it's an unsolvable maze.

I look in the mirror and hardly recognize the person there. The pain is etched on his tired face; the lines under his eyes are deeper than this time last year. Overweight from his medications, he wonders if anyone realizes how self-conscious he feels these days in front of people. He tries his best to hide it.

These days, he is giving more away than he has. There simply aren't many more reserve tanks.

"How can you stay so joyous all the time?" people ask.

"I don't," I reply, with all the honesty I can muster. "I really struggle, too."

And then they say, "Oh, you are so modest."

Later, as I prepare to board yet another airplane, the lady at the counter reads my ticket and says, "Have a good trip, Mr. Hansel."

For a second I'm caught by surprise. It's my name—but there is no living resonance—she doesn't know me. She didn't even look at my face, only at my ticket. How can she know my deepest hurts and joys? I'm only a name in a stack of tickets.

The strange paradox is that as our world grows ever more crowded, we grow ever more lonely.

    FROM MY JOURNAL:
Just tell the truth—as you know it—
always. It is the only thing that will set
you free. And the truth is that the pain has
almost broken me. I sometimes feel so
inadequate—unable to be the person I
want to be.

Oh, loneliness. Everyone knows what that
is like. —T. S. ELIOT

BUT SOME PEOPLE ARE never lonely, right? Like extroverts—they're never lonely. And how could married people know the pain of loneliness? Surely beautiful people aren't ever lonely. And successful people—they don't even have time to be lonely.

Isn't it amazing that at times we actually think this way? The media would have us believe that there are certain people who have somehow missed the anguish and confusion that loneliness brings to the rest of us.

Kathy is the mother of two happy, healthy children, married to an IBM executive who is outrageously successful. What reason would she have for ever being lonely? Yet in a conversation recently she described an unexpected void in her life, a hole in her soul that nothing seemed to fill. As Kathy described her loneliness, her words ached with that feeling of isolation.

    FROM MY JOURNAL:
Lately I have experienced a loneliness so deep that I feel as though I need a second heart to contain all the pain. A deep sense of dislocation overwhelms my very being. I feel disconnected from all that I treasure— God, my family, my friends, even myself. Perhaps this is at the heart of loneliness, a great feeling of disconnection. A floundering feeling of helpless aloneness. Loneliness can be so paralyzing. Its vague, pervasive power invades every cell and fills it with cement.

I was sitting alone in a restaurant. A little boy was crying. His mom lifted him gently, placed her lips on his tummy and blew vigorously. He giggled and laughed. I think that's what I need.

In the midst of our loneliness, we often feel like we're the only ones. But the truth is that to be human is to know loneliness firsthand. Although each of us is as unique as our fingerprints, we have all known at times the ache of loneliness. It is part of the human condition.

> *And He saw the Spirit of God descending like a dove, and lighting upon Him: And lo a voice from heaven, saying, This is My beloved Son, in whom I am well pleased. Then was Jesus led up of the Spirit into the wilderness. . . .* —MATTHEW 3:16b—4:1 (KJV)

THIS PASSAGE OF SCRIPTURE has always been slightly confusing for me. Jesus has just been baptized. A holy dove has descended from heaven to endorse Him as the Son of God. The heavens have opened. The place is in awe. Folks are stunned. Excited. Expectant. The Messiah they've been awaiting for centuries has just been announced. Jesus is ready to begin His public ministry. What will God do next?

What God did next is unexpected, to say the least. He said, "This is my beloved Son in whom I'm well pleased." And then He immediately sent Him into the wilderness to undergo loneliness, hunger, hardship, and temptation.

Isn't it interesting that the way the Father showed His love for Jesus, His only Son, was to put Him in the desert, so that at the critical beginning of His ministry He would learn to depend on the Father . . . alone?

Perhaps one of the reasons God nudges each of us into a desert of some kind is so that we will learn to depend on Him in new ways.

> *Again and again they scoff, 'Where is that God of yours?' But O my soul, don't be discouraged. Don't be upset. Expect God to act! . . . For you are God, my only place of refuge.* —PSALM 42:10b, 11; 43:2a (TLB)

C.S. LEWIS SAID that God whispers to us in our joys, speaks to us in our conscience, and shouts to us in our pain. In our joys, it is as though He is whispering in a crowded auditorium of His immense, outrageous love for us—but we can't hear. We're too busy. We're too enmeshed with our friends, our joys, our lives.

He tries again to speak to us through our conscience, but we don't slow down enough to listen. Our hearing aid is on low, because we're engaged with so many things. Without purposeful listening, the communication process is not complete.

But the Hound of Heaven is persistent in His love and concern, so He shouts . . . through pain. He finally has our attention.

And in the pain of our loneliness He says, "You are My child in whom I'm well pleased. Now I'm going to lead you through the desert so that you can taste Me, touch Me, see Me, hear Me in new ways."

Loneliness is not a time of abandonment . . . it just feels that way. It's actually a time of encounter at new levels with the only One who can fill that empty place in our hearts.

Loneliness need not be an enemy . . . it can be a friend.

Loneliness need not be an interruption in our lives . . . it can be a gift.

Loneliness need not be an obstacle . . . it can be an invitation.

Loneliness need not be a problem . . . it can be an opportunity.

Loneliness need not be a dead end . . . it can be an adventure!

As Clark Moustakas says: "Loneliness leaves its traces in man but these are marks of pathos, of weathering, which enhance dignity and maturity and love. . . . Loneliness is as much a reality of life as night and rain and thunder and it can be lived creatively. So I say let there be loneliness, for where there is loneliness, there is also sensitivity, there is awareness and recognition of promise."

The human drama does not show itself on the surface of life; it is not played out in the visible world, but in the hearts of men and women. —ANTOINE DE SAINT EXUPÉRY

IT HAS BEEN OBSERVED that if our lives were only sunshine, they would be a desert. I have reflected on that thought many times, and I know somehow we are called to a firm meaning in spite of all the tragedies about us and within us. God wants to plant a tree in our desert. He wants to create a garden in our wilderness, an oasis where we can again be refreshed.

Many people still choose to numb themselves to the pain, to be distracted, to put on insulation, to seek escapes—to somehow avoid the pain. But if we are to discover the depth of solitude in the heart of loneliness, we cannot continually go around the pain. To the best of our abilities we must wade through the emotions that we experience, no matter what the cost. Our God will use these painful times to draw us into deeper intimacy with Him.

I recall a time in my life when I went through a trough so deep that I thought I would need a ladder just to get to the bottom of the well. Fortunately I had some friends who walked through that valley with me. At one point, when I was ready to give up, Craig did the most surprising thing. He grabbed me by the shirt collar, shook me, and said, "Tim, less than two percent of the world's population ever gets to know life at this level. You have got to go through it. I'm not going to let you stop, and I'm not going to let you go around it. We'll go through this thing no matter how painful it is. The way out is through."

❧ *FROM MY JOURNAL:*
> *I asked my Lord*
> > *In the midst of it all,*
> > > *"How do I find my way out?"*
> > *And He replied,*
> > > *"One step at a time, my son,*
> > > *One step at a time."*

> *He delights in each step they take.*
> > —PSALM 37:23 (TLB)

> *When you tell me, then I'll know what my*
> *next step should be, whether to move this*
> *way or that.* —GENESIS 24:49 (TLB)

In *Winning Life's Toughest Battles*, Dr. Julias Segal writes poignantly of the importance of taking action, no matter how small, in times of great stress and difficulty. The more difficult the trouble, he says, the more important it is to take some small step—to act, and, hence, reduce your feelings of hopelessness and powerlessness.

Persons traumatized by crisis often feel cut off not only from their past, but from their future as well. They become disoriented and feel lost. When one is mired in such a crisis, Segal insists that the smallest action can be the key to survival. He relates a story about a traveler in northern Vermont who was convinced he was on the wrong road. He stopped his car, rolled down the window, and said to a passerby, "Friend, I need help. I'm lost."

The villager looked at him a moment and said, "Do you know where you are?"

"Yes," said the traveler. "I saw the name of the village when I entered."

The man nodded his head. "Do you know where you want to be?"

"Yes," the traveler replied, and named his destination.

The villager looked away for a moment and then said, "You ain't lost. You just need directions."[1]

Frequently when we are overwhelmed by loneliness, we feel lost and powerless. Sometimes we feel that we can no longer endure it, but we can't escape it. Our search for God, for others, and even for ourselves ends only in silence. Sometimes the worst part of loneliness is feeling out of control, like a helpless victim. We feel like we are at the mercy of others, and we constantly wait for someone else to act. Little do we realize that there are countless little steps that we can take. We "ain't lost" . . . we "just need directions."

Segal relates story after story of people who took charge of their lives even in the most dire circumstances. Some were hostages. Some were POWs. Some endured unbelievable trauma. But the common denominator among them was their courage to act. No matter how small the action, it gave them a sense of victory.

Patti Blumenthal does exceptional work with kids from the probation department. These kids have no shortage of problems and difficulties. One day when she was telling me about her work, she kept using some initials that were unfamiliar to me. After the third or fourth time, my curiosity got the best of me.

"All right, Patti," I said, "what's this NTS?"

With great delight she explained, "Oh, that's the Next Tiny Step. These kids can't take big steps, but they can take tiny ones."

This concept has had a profound impact on my life. It has been of inestimable value, especially during times of difficulty. It has helped me realize that I can always initiate some change, no matter how small. God doesn't ask us to take big steps . . . just the next tiny step.

In this book you will notice an occasional entry designated "NTS." These are to remind us that even with a problem like loneliness, there is a need to be practical, to exercise some control. When we have a sense of doing something, no matter how small, we realize that we are not paralyzed. We can still move. We can still make life happen.

Take some action. There is no substitute for experience. Take time to respond to the NTS suggestions and then create some of your own. Loneliness can sometimes feel like a loose thread unraveling the tattered fabric of our lives. The NTS sections will remind us that we always have some place to go.

One of the soundest pieces of advice I was ever given is this:

*Do the very best you can
with what you have
where you are now.*

I AM CAUGHT IN L.A. TRAFFIC. (Could L.A. stand for Loneliness Anonymous?) What an amazing paradox. There are people all around me, yet I feel so alone. All of them are encased in their own thoughts and feelings. We stop and start and pass each other by without even noticing. Radios blare, but there is no communication between us. We sit here, stiff and solitary. Each lost in a private world. Stopping and starting and stopping again.

I'm suffocated by all the people, yet stifled by my own loneliness. Bumper-to-bumper sadness. Bumper-to-bumper loneliness. How strange that as the world grows ever more heavily populated, our depth of loneliness increases.

To ease the pain of loneliness, there must be connection.

Connection with ourselves. Connection with others. A felt experience with God. The night settles over the freeway. Headlights pinpoint the silhouette in front and behind and on each side.

We sit encased in mobile tombstones, sealed off from each other. The doors are locked from the inside. We do it to ourselves. We limit our own ability to reach out to each other. Taillights blink on, shouting, "Don't touch me. Leave me alone."

In our hurried entrapment, we see each other only through masks and windshields. Our antennas are up. We fight for our space. In the midst of this hurried stream of loneliness, we are quite assuredly the lonely crowd. A mass of isolated people who are more perplexed and hardened. We have more sophisticated techniques than ever before in history, but no communication—no connection. We seem lost, weaving from one lane to the next, struggling to get home. Shouting at the car in front of us but never heard . . . never heard. How strange to feel almost claustrophobic from the crowdedness of all the people . . . yet be so desperately alone.

The odometer on our lives keeps turning over. We need not repair, not a mere tune-up, but restoration. Transformation. We need more than just to fill our tanks. We need to discover a cup that ever overflows. We need more than just our windshields cleaned— we need new eyes.

I pray also that the eyes of your heart may be enlightened in order that you may know the hope to which he has called you, the riches of his glorious inheritance in the saints, and his incomparably great power for us who believe. —EPHESIANS 1:18, 19a

With All My Heart

Jesus died to take away our sins, not our feelings.

I have often marveled at how we humans so value the spiritual and cognitive aspects of our person while devaluing the emotional aspect—as if God, when He was creating human beings, only got two-thirds of it right.　　　　—DAVID NORTON

We arrive at truth not by reason alone, but also by the heart.　　　　—BLAISE PASCAL

TO DENY YOUR FEELINGS is to deny a great portion of yourself. It's very hard, if not impossible, to be real if you're repressing the emotional side of your being. We were made in the image of God—and that includes a whole spectrum of feelings.

Dr. David Viscott says, "Our feelings are our sixth sense, the sense that interprets, arranges, directs, and summarizes the other five. Feelings tell us whether what we experience is threatening, painful, sad, or joyous. Feelings can be described and explained in simple and direct ways. . . . Feelings make up a language all their own. When feelings speak, we are compelled to listen and sometimes act—even if we do not always understand why. Not to be aware of one's feelings, not to understand them or know how to use or express them is worse than being blind, deaf, or paralyzed. Not to feel is not to be alive. More than anything else, feelings make us human. Feelings make us all kindred."[2]

Feelings are a source of energy. Feelings are messages. They help us know who and where we are. When we lose touch with our feelings, we lose touch with that which makes us human.

We serve a God of great feelings, great passion; you can't miss that in Scripture. The Book is crammed with feelings. The same God who listened to Job's agony, to Jonah's wailing, to Elijah's depression, and to the psalmist's pain and struggles is ready to listen to us. God is definitely not fragile when it comes to hearing our deepest emotions.

Someone, somewhere, once told us "not to think with our feelings." That's good advice. When we think with our emotions we can get very confused. But what many of us heard was "don't feel our feelings." We heard "it's not okay to get upset, to feel lonely, to get frustrated, to feel emotional pain." But what we don't realize is that by repressing these painful feelings, we put a lid on positive feelings as well. It's no wonder we struggle to feel all the love and joy and peace that we would like to feel.

Perhaps there is no such thing as "good" or "bad" feelings. Feelings are simply our responses to information, truth, and experience. And when we simply learn to feel our feelings—to identify them clearly and express them accurately—we cannot only stop negative patterns but feel the power of joy that is our promise.

Our Christian walk is made up of at least three parts: fact, faith, and feelings. These are like a three-legged stool. If you pull one leg away, the stool will fall over. Feelings are a part of any love relationship, even our relationship with God. Feelings are what keep the relationship alive. We must know God with our heart as well as with our head.

Sometimes life is like words and music . . .
that can't seem to become a song.

ANNE WAS RAISED in a home where the expression of real feelings was taboo. She could smile and be content, but to be excessive in her joy was not acceptable. Likewise anger was not ladylike, and loneliness meant you weren't letting God love you. She was supposed to be a "good girl"—obedient, submissive, and thoughtful. She was definitely not allowed to "color outside the lines."

She says, "The boundaries were very rigid. We knew what we were supposed to feel—and that was about it. Any feelings outside the norm were strictly forbidden. Therefore, I grew up wondering what to do with these 'other feelings.' Usually I just ignored them or denied them. The problem is that eventually they began coming out all over the place—in ailments, doubts, frustrations, anger, depression, and the like."

Now in her forties, the mother of two children, Anne has known her share of frustration. One day she said to her husband, "There is a whole washing machine full of feelings going on inside of me, and I can't sort them out. They just roll around inside of me until I feel like I'm going to explode."

Her husband helped her give herself permission to explore those feelings and begin to try to convey them to others. It has saved their marriage. And because she is now free to explore her feelings, she in turn is encouraging her children to get in touch with their feelings. They are learning early on the "language of feelings," how to identify emotions and give them accurate expression—so they won't be controlled by them.

🔖 *FROM MY JOURNAL:*
You can't laugh if you don't feel.
You can't know true joy unless you've cried.

M Y BIBLE HAS PAGES which are crammed and overflowing with a passionate God who seeks out His people—and men and women who loved Him passionately in return.

My Bible says that David was a man of great emotion, that Mary Magdalene loved Jesus with all her heart, that Moses thundered with passion in all he did, that Paul caused a fervor on more than one occasion, that Peter didn't make little mistakes— and that God loves His people with great passion.

Emotions are a gift from God, given to us so we can respond to life. The problem with feelings is that you really have to feel them. You can't heal what you can't feel. As one of my defense mechanisms, I learned how to think "about" feelings and talk "about" feelings rather than really feel them. The two are galaxies apart. Maybe the worst mistake we can make is to repress our feelings instead of learning how to properly express them. Perhaps without knowing it, we are cutting off God's ability to work in us.

I also learned how to dress up my unacceptable feelings so as to make them look good. I learned to disguise them so cleverly that sometimes I didn't even realize they were only imitation feelings. It's only another form of denial.

Feelings are real—they need to be experienced and shared—but they are not always accurate. We must constantly balance our feelings against the truths revealed in Scripture.

But how do we begin to free up our feelings? Some of us have chosen safe "clip-on" feelings—flat, nonthreatening, and two-dimensional—that really come from our heads. But that process keeps feelings frozen within us, bogged down, a tundra of thick, opaque, inflexible emotions that can't be thawed out.

Some of us have learned "cookie cutter" feelings with clean edges—that are often borrowed from someone else and are not our own. The result is they are glued on like a postage stamp and tend to come off in the flurry of everyday life. They are nice, bland, antiseptic, thimble-size feelings which are okay for a church picnic but inadequate for a relationship of any depth, even with yourself—and especially with God.

Real feelings that come from the holy furnace within us are sometimes dangerous, difficult, exciting, and passionate. They are both gentle and bold, subtle and surprising, delicate and over-whelming—unadulterated by overevaluation.

Feelings will always find a way to be "ex-pressed" (pushed out). We can lie to ourselves, and even to God, but we cannot lie to our bodies. Our bodies will always end up telling the truth about our repressed feelings. If we do not ex-press them (push them out), these feelings will come out in some way through our body—tense muscles, headaches, backaches, ulcers, depression, fatigue, or various other symptoms.

The mind and the body are one. What you do physically will affect you mentally and emotionally. We've heard that so many times it has lost its power. But it's true. "For as he thinketh in his heart, so is he" (Proverbs 23:7, KJV).

One of the best things we can do amidst difficult feelings is strenuous exercise. Stretch your body. Stretch your emotions. Stretch your spirit. Stretch your mind. The greatest releasers of emotions are prayer and exercise. They are God's design to help us let go of frustration.

I know some people who, while going through difficult emotions, have taken their time of struggle as an opportunity to improve their physical fitness—and in doing so they impacted their emotional state in a positive way. Hear it again: the mind and the body are one. And when you exercise at a gym or a fitness center, you'll probably be around some new people; serendipitously, you may begin to impact your loneliness from a new angle.

Often times I try to go around the difficult emotions—but they will come back and find some way to find expression. Knowing this I have decided to learn how to wade through my own wilderness of emotions, no matter how painful. It requires a difficult and deeper kind of courage—but what an adventure!

➡ *NTS:*

So go ahead: get physical with your emotions. Use the large muscles of your body; do aerobics, cycle, run, walk! The more frustrated you are by your feelings, the more you need to stretch yourself physically.

Treat yourself to a new pair of running shorts— the brighter the better. Move. Take charge. Don't just sit back and wait for an answer. Make something happen today. Do five minutes of exercise. It all begins with a tiny step.

The strongest and the brightest of us are fragile as a floating bubble, unsteady as a newborn kitten on a waxed kitchen floor.

—LEWIS SMEDES

SOME YEARS AGO a delightful movie came out entitled *Short Circuit*. It was a story of a robot that got struck by lightning and came "alive." Because of his robotic skills, he could accomplish incredible feats and absorb massive amounts of information. He learns the English language by watching TV and reading. He quotes John Wayne or Shakespeare and numerous others in his attempts to figure out what life is all about.

At one point it is said of him, "Johnny Five is making a lot of mistakes—because he is alive." Being a "live robot" introduces him to all the frailties of being alive and human. In the sequel, *Short Circuit II*, Johnny Five discovers what it means to be rejected. As he travels out on the streets, people don't know what to do with him and, in their confusion, reject him. He says to his friend Ben, "What is this feeling, this emotion? It feels hollow, empty, like a desert. I am now feeling lower than down. I realize that not even a crowd is company, and I'm feeling very lonely."

His friend Ben says, "Being alive is very difficult. Human beings are very complicated. I know. I spent my whole life being one, and I still can't figure it out."

Johnny Five discovers that being alive involves all sorts of complications that he didn't anticipate. Because he has feelings, he is prone to loneliness.

This movie makes me think of a piece that I was given some time ago called "Chronically Human." It was written in the form of a memo:

To Whom It May Concern:

I am chronically human. If the following signs are observed, I am not emotionally disturbed or dying.

1. If you find me stumbling and falling, I may be trying something new—I am learning.

2. If you find me sad, I may have realized that I have been making the same mistakes again and again—I am exploring.

3. If you find me frightened, I may be in a new situation—I am reaching out.

4. If you find me crying, I may have failed—I am lonely.

5. If you find me very quiet. I may be planning— I am trying again.

These are life signs of beings of my nature. If prolonged absence of the above indicators is observed, do not perform an autopsy without first providing an opportunity and invitation for life to emerge.   —Bob L. Means

God has made us human beings in His image with the need for His fellowship. At

*the same time He has created us with a
need for other people. Thus loneliness may
reflect a deficiency in either or both of
these directions.* —ELIZABETH SKOGLUND

To BE HUMAN MEANS that you will sometimes be lonely. Being lonely is not unspiritual. Being lonely is not sinful or weak. We were made for relationships, and when those relationships are not intact, we are designed to experience loneliness.

Many of our biblical heroes experienced loneliness.

Elijah, frustrated after his great conquest over the gods of Baal, cried out, "I am the only one." Abraham must have felt incredibly alone when he was asked to sacrifice his only son, Isaac. Moses knew what it was to feel alone, and through that discovered a God that he wanted to know personally—and who wanted to know him personally. The apostle Paul cried out, "Send me Barnabas!" to ease the pain of his loneliness. Even Jesus Himself knew loneliness on more than one occasion.

As He approached the Garden of Gethsemane, Jesus said to His disciples, "Sit here while I go over there and pray." He took three of the disciples with Him when He went into the heart of the garden. He said to them, "My soul is overwhelmed with sorrow to the point of death. Stay here and keep watch with Me" (Matthew 26:36, 37).

Going a little farther, He fell facedown upon the ground and prayed that the Father would take this cup from Him; yet He prayed, "Not as I will, but as You will, Father." As He returned from that prayer, He found His three closest friends asleep. "Could you not watch with Me for one hour?" He asked. He who was fully God was fully human and knew the need for human and divine companionship at the deepest levels. Shortly after this incredibly lonely moment, one of His disciples betrayed Him.

Yes, He fully understands our loneliness. In fact, perhaps the loneliest statement ever offered was Jesus' cry from the cross, "My God, my God, why have you forsaken me?" (Matthew 27:46).

I think that these experiences were written about in Scripture to remind us not to fear loneliness, but to have the courage to go through it. The way out is through!

➡ *NTS:*

Remember: God is greater than any problem that you have. Write out the following verse on a three-by-five card and tape it onto your bathroom mirror or place it on your kitchen sink.

"So, humble yourselves under God's strong hand, and in His own good time He will lift you up. You can throw the whole weight of your anxieties upon Him, for you are His personal concern" (I Peter 5: 6, 7, Phillips).

Images and Emptiness

Be kind. Remember that everyone you
meet is fighting a hard battle.
—T. H. THOMPSON

For He has given laughter in my sadness
and colored rainbows with my pain.
—SHELLY CHAPIN

SOMETIMES I FEEL lonely because I feel unacceptable. My body has changed. Some of the medications that I take to try and stop the ever-increasing pain have caused me to gain some unnecessary and unwanted weight. It's really interesting to see how people respond to me when I get off the plane to do a speaking engagement.

"You look different from your picture," a young man said recently. "I expected someone—well, I don't know how to say it."

I tried to help him out. "I know. After reading *Holy Sweat*, you expected someone younger and leaner."

"How old are you, anyway?" he asked.

We live in an age of images. I know that people read my books and get a certain image of me. They read *You Gotta Keep Dancin'* and, though I never said so in the book, think I have somehow mastered the pain.

Just the other night a lady said to me, "How do you do it?"

And I had to respond, "I don't. I am fighting for my very dignity right now. I'm struggling just to keep the boat upright."

The tears in her eyes gave evidence that hearing this was probably what she needed—not hearing how somebody has whipped the pain and conquered it totally.

You and I are simply fellow strugglers. None of us has our life or our pain in control, although we sometimes try to pretend that we do.

Even great success does not automatically preclude loneliness. Ernest Hemingway, at the peak of his career, said, "I live in a vacuum that is as lonely as a radio tube when the batteries are dead and there is no current to plug into."

Each weekend I meet wonderful people—but people whom I will only know for a short period of time. I relish the spontaneity and joy of those new relationships, but I ache with a longing for belonging that dissipates as I get on the plane to fly home. At home, I feel sometimes that Pam and the boys have somehow learned to function without me, perhaps too well. Sometimes I feel like a stranger in my own home. Coming in and going out again, not having that essential primal ingredient that is so vital in a relationship—time. Long-distance relationships lack that physical presence that you can see across the table. That spontaneity of change and growth when people are together for long periods of time; a continuity of relationships that creates the kind of depth where you no longer need words; that music of friendship that sings in its own key.

Yet, I am grateful that all of this has forced me to depend on God in deeper and stronger ways. St. Augustine's oft-repeated statement is still true: "O Lord, my heart is restless until it finds its rest in Thee." God, too, must ache with our restlessness. I wonder if He, too, doesn't long to find His rest in us. And there are so few people these days in whom He can find rest.

In the midst of my bewilderment, I am struggling to be one of those people. If we are not afraid of our loneliness, it can lead us to dimensions of our lives that we never knew existed before. If we will allow our loneliness to teach us, we will discover again that we are truly not alone—we can know an Inner Presence and hope that transcends anything that a mere mortal can give.

Loneliness reminds us that we were made by God—for God— that our loneliness can be transformed into solitude, which can and will teach us about genuine, inextinguishable love. As Mike Mason says so well, "In each one of us the holiest and neediest place of all has been reserved for God alone, so that only He can enter there. No one else can love us as He does, and no one else can be the sort of Friend to us that He is."

When we're in the presence of another person, we're on holy ground; God is at work in that person, too. —EUGENE PETERSON

IN THE INDIAN LANGUAGE there is a greeting, *Namaste*, which means "I honor the holy one who lives within you."

Loneliness stems in a large part from not honoring the holy one who lives within us. If you have invited Christ into your life, I believe He does in fact dwell within you. Likewise, we must learn how to honor the holy one within each other, so that we do not seek to use people simply to fill our emptiness.

Our world has a distorted view of love, in that we sometimes expect one other person to meet and fill all our needs. No human being, no matter what the relationship, meets all the needs of another person. If you are seeking to fill your tank through human relationships only, you are destined to a certain amount of emptiness.

Like a headlight that can only reach so far into the darkness, human love by its very nature has its limits. Our focus instead needs to be on the One who said, "I am the way, the truth, and the life."

We need to stop looking for certainty in order to discover truth. By its very nature, life has the capacity and propensity to change.

We sometimes assume that God is leading toward a prearranged goal. He may not be. What He desires most from us is obedience. Surrender to His person. Sensitivity to His presence.

Our God is a God of history and a God of the future, but He lives in the present tense. His name is "I Am," not "I Was" or "I Will Be." There is a certain kind of loneliness when we try to live in the past or the future. When we want the next moment to have something that this moment doesn't. A certain kind of peace invades us when we realize that this moment is complete in and of itself. That this moment is sacred. That this moment is enough. That this moment is not lacking in anything that we need.

➡ *NTS:*

> I don't wear glasses—yet. But I have a pair of glasses frames that mean a lot to me. Twenty-five years ago I got the idea of putting on these frames with no glass in them just as a reminder to me to "see the world through Christ's eyes."

Get a pair of glasses frames or, if you wear glasses, put a piece of tape on the side of your lens as a reminder to see the world through Christ's eyes. Wear the glasses or the tape for whatever period of time fits for you, and really make an effort to see the world as you think Christ would see it. It will change not only the way you see people, but the way you treat them. Someone once said, "People will forget what you say, people will forget what you did, but people will never forget how you made them feel."

As for learning to live in the present, I have found a very simple way to help me do that. I place a rubber band on my wrist as a reminder to live in this instant. When I am having real trouble doing that, I reach down and snap the rubber band as a frisky reminder. God lives in the present tense. It is here that we can know Him most fully.

ॐ *FROM MY JOURNAL:*
Real love requires time, exposure, vulnerability, and commitment. The same is true of our relationship with God. If our

love relationship with God is to grow, we must be ruthlessly honest with Him and let Him be ruthlessly honest with us. We must above all give Him time—time in which we can expose the real core of our being. We must dare to be real and open and vulnerable with Him.

TIME AND AGAIN I come back to a single verse, Psalm 23:1. "The Lord is my shepherd; I shall not be in want." I shall not be found lacking. I shall not be left empty or hopeless. I shall not be found wanting. God is consistent in this theme throughout the Bible, and I am practicing to make this principle consistent in my life. The here and now is enough.

I can trust God with my future, which not only means eternal life, but the next day, the next hour, the next ten minutes. Filling our emptiness is an inside-out job. It means letting Him fill our loneliness with a fullness that we will never comprehend and only He can give.

Advertisements shout, "You need more. Your life is not enough." God whispers in the midst, "I am here. I am sufficient in your weakness. I am enough. In Me you are complete."

In Christ there is an uncrowded fullness. In Him there is an unhurried completeness. In Him is a whole number. In Him, enough is enough.

> *Then shalt thou call, and the Lord shall*
> *answer; thou shalt cry, and he shall say,*
> *Here I am . . . And the Lord shall guide*
> *thee continually, and satisfy thy soul in*
> *drought . . . and thou shalt be like a*
> *watered garden, and like a spring of*
> *water, whose waters fail not.*
> —ISAIAH 58:9a, 11 (KJV)

➤ *NTS:*

When was the last time you actually memorized a verse of Scripture? Commit this one to memory, and ask God to bring it to your mind throughout the remainder of this day.

"My grace is sufficient for you, for my power is made perfect in weakness" (II Corinthians 12:9).

Change takes place because we're fully accepted, not because we're strong. Make friends with your weaknesses. Identify five and thank God for them, because they will be opportunities for His power to be displayed.

Where Is God?

Our God remains a hidden God, but in prayer we discover that we have what we seek. —BRENNAN MANNING

I WAS RAISED IN SEATTLE. Once when I was little, our Boy Scout troop went to Bainbridge Island for a weekend camp-out. On the second day we had a ferocious game of hide-and-seek. I discovered a great hiding place in the ivy next to the big house. I crawled in along the wall and squeezed myself behind the ivy so I was completely camouflaged. When the seekers came so close I could almost touch them, I held my breath. It was exciting because I could watch them looking for me.

The problem came when they got tired and stopped looking for me. They just gave up. I kept thinking, "They just haven't tried hard enough. They're all looking for me far away, when I'm right here. If they would only look right under their noses, they would find me."

I resorted to making some subtle noises to give them hints, but they still didn't spot me. It was as though they were refusing to look for me up close—it was too obvious. Finally I hung my red bandanna out on one of the branches. Jeremy, a kid I didn't know very well, found the bandanna . . . but never saw me.

Forty-some years later, I realize what a picture this is of much of our lives. Often we don't find what we're looking for because we don't look at what is close to us. We don't find God because we are only looking for Him in faraway places. God is hidden in our midst, if we could only see Him.

How close is God? Philippians 4:5 says, "Never forget the nearness of your Lord." He is closer than your breath. He is closer than your skin. How much does He care for us? Scripture reminds us:

He knows our names (John 10:3).

He numbers the hairs of our head (Matthew 10:30).

He counts the steps of our feet (Job 14:16).

He knows our thoughts (Psalm 139:2).

He bottles the tears from our eyes (Psalm 56:8).

He holds our right hands in His hand (Psalm 73:23).

He supplies all our needs (Philippians 4:19).

Many believers don't seek God in such things as loneliness, despair, depression, or anxiety—because God is "hidden" in these things. It's just too hard, and we're looking for easy answers. We will only see Him in these "close" areas of our lives if we seek Him there.

➡ *NTS:*

> Where are you missing God in your life? In which areas of your life are you having the most difficulty finding His presence and promise? Are you able to recognize His work in and through you in the midst of your loneliness or in the midst of some crisis you are facing? Write down ten places or areas of your life where you may be overlooking Him.
>
> As the psalmist says, "I am always thinking of the Lord; and because He is so near, I never need to stumble or to fall." (Psalm 16:8, TLB)
>
> Finally (and I hope this is as powerful for you as it has been for me) read Psalm 139 (preferably in *The Living Bible*) slowly and carefully, absorbing the incredible truth that you can never get away from God even if you try.

LONELINESS IS NOT the same as being alone. Loneliness is feeling alone . . . no matter how many people are around you. It is a feeling of being disconnected, unplugged, left out, isolated. We're surrounded daily with images of the "good life," and we feel as though we've missed it completely.

Loneliness is one of those emotions that doesn't just exist by itself. It hitchhikes off guilt and depression. It is a parasite to host emotions like fear and sadness. It clings tenaciously to feelings like anxiety and makes us feel that things are all wrong, when they may be all right.

Unfortunately, you can't buy anything over the counter to cure it. You can't heal it by reading a book. You can't drive away from it in your car or hop on a plane and fly to a new solution.

Loneliness occurs deep down within us, and the only hope for a solution must also come from that deep down suchness of a place and a Person. Through conversation and presence we can turn loneliness into something powerful. Prayer is our means of conversation with God, and solitude is our opportunity for experiencing His inner presence. And how do we experience His presence? We must stop to recognize how near He is.

Our associate pastor was working as a camp counselor of junior high boys one summer. One night he was coming back to the cabin and, as he approached, heard an uproar that was probably audible in the next state. He walked up and stood in the doorway a few moments, silently observing the rambunctious pillow fight taking place. Then he heard one of the kids say, "He's coming. He's coming. He's coming!," the boy's voice getting louder and louder as he tried to warn the others of the impending presence of their counselor.

There was a pause, and then one of the kids saw him in the doorway and said, "He's here! He's h-e-r-e!"

What a wonderful illustration of our relationships with God. Many Christians proclaim frequently "He's coming! He's coming!" . . . but they fail to recognize that He's here. He is here. Present in beauty. Present in the lives of other believers. Present in His Church. Present in the needs of the world. He is here . . . if we can but recognize His presence.

➤ *NTS:*

Find a friend and "brainstorm" five to ten ways to experience God's presence in practical ways. Jesus said, "I have come that they may have life, and have it to the full." (John 10:10) Saint Irenaeus said, "The glory of God is man fully alive." Write down a list of those things that make you feel most alive, and see if you can find His presence there.

ONE OF THE REASONS we are so paralyzed in our attempts to reach out and reach in stems from the American dream of having it all together. We pretend to be more whole, more attractive than we really are in the hope that it will invite a greater acceptance from others and somehow heal our loneliness.

The level of our emotional pain is in direct proportion to how much we are covering up. We have repressed our feelings for so long that they now strain, push, and shove to no avail. Even our prayers have swollen tongues. Our heart is a dust bowl of unfenced feelings whirling across the barrenness of our soul.

Many of us are drowning in our own emptiness, not realizing that this is a very invitation to be filled by an ever-present God, a God who loves us more than we will ever understand or experience. But a loneliness which is not fully embraced and experienced will break you and haunt you. Trying to avoid it only makes it more powerful. The more you run and hide, the more it will pursue you— until it finds you and swallows you whole. It is relentless, stalking.

Our thin porcelain shell of pride insists that we are too spiritually and socially mature to have to engage in something so mundane as loneliness. Hence, its subtle invasion in our lives can be read on our faces, our eyes, our paleness, and our whole posture even if we refuse to let the word cross our lips.

Little do we realize that our quest for peace must go through the loneliness. All of us will have our own paths. Some are just longer than others. Some wider. Some with more stones and obstacles. But not to walk the path is to get lost.

> *The cross is the gift God gives His friends.*
> —MYLES CONNELLY

> *Pain is often the sign that prayer is being answered.*
> —ROBERT HERHOLD

I TALKED TO AN ARCHITECT once about the magnificence of tall skyscrapers. Curiously I asked him how high they can go. His answer surprised me.

"Tim, it's not how high they can go, but how deep they can go. For every floor that goes up, you must have a floor that goes down as well to counterbalance it."

And I thought how our lives in Christ can only go as high as we are willing to go deep. Going deep requires time, thoughtfully digging into who we are and who God really is. Loneliness is like a buried cache which promises sustenance for the journey . . . but we've got to dig for it. The more suffocating the loneliness, the deeper we have to dig.

What is your capacity for God? How deep are you willing to dig? Too many of us experience shallow relationships with God because we are unwilling to do the hard work that is necessary. Building a relationship, like building a skyscraper, takes time.

I want to dig a canyon in my relationship with God . . . but more often it seems I have only dug a trough.

➡ *NTS:*

George Herbert once said, "Thou who has given me so much, give me one thing more—a grateful heart." Nothing makes us feel separate from God more than what has sometimes been called the ugliest of sins, ingratitude. But on the opposite side, nothing creates more intimacy with God than genuine gratitude. Are you spending time alone with Him reading Scripture, praying, and sometimes just listening to what He wants to say to you? What are five words that describe your spiritual life right now? If you had a shovel, in what areas of your life would you start digging in order to create a deeper relationship with God? It takes hard work. Nothing comes easy.

*I have learned the true meaning of words
like love, pain, endurance, and devotion.
I've learned that God doesn't want part of
me, He wants all of me.*

—SUMMIT PARTICIPANT

SOMETIMES THE GREATEST lessons we learn in life come as a surprise. We didn't expect them. We didn't intend them. They are another one of those serendipitous gifts from God.

In Acts 1:8 we are called to *be* His witnesses. It implies that we not only speak the message, we *are* the message. Who we are radiates so loudly that people frequently can't hear what we say.

I had a quiet but profound experience one Saturday when I was asked to speak to 350 women at a luncheon. I shared the platform with a quiet woman of simple stature. Janice Sakuma had lost her eleven-year-old daughter to a dreaded disease. Yet in the midst of her pain she radiated a peace that I have rarely seen or experienced. I was so touched by her radiant peace in God in spite of painful circumstances that I went home and wrote the following in my journal: "A question seeks an answer like a right seeks a left and an up finds a down—like the inside melts into an outside. Like one hand finds another to clap. Like a foot finds the earth to walk.

"So my restless soul was looking, without knowing it, for that peace that passes all understanding. I didn't even know I was looking until I saw the answer. It was not a theory, not a concept, not an abstract complexity . . . but a life. I didn't know I was that restless, that my life was that noisy, that the pain had driven me so far into the corner of distress until I encountered You in a simple, beautiful, Japanese mother who had lost her daughter.

"She was simply a coat for Your presence. Her pain had driven her to the point where she had let go, opened up her hands, and let You fill her. Her voice was Your voice. Her smile was Your smile. Her peace was Your peace.

"I felt like a shag rug in the presence of a king. My worn edges ragged, my matting worn thin by years of overuse. I was honored— and embarrassed—to be in Your presence.

"I felt like a raging river next to a deep, still pond. A sanctuary, a refuge. I think for the first time I saw the meaning of those biblical words, 'You are my refuge, my hiding place. I am in You and You are in me. You are my fortress and my salvation.' "

Janice in her simple, humble way showed me what God is really like. She was simply a believer. Most work and work and work to tune their lives to the harmony of God. She simply let go.

I don't know who influenced whom, but Janice's daughter, Stefanie, had an uncommon maturity at the age of nine. She wrote a book of poetry which was published after her death. Here is one of her poems, called "Hope."

It is only when you seek
That you find
Some light and hope
In a wall behind.

Don't always let walls stand in the way.
In your journey looking for
A hope or a light
Keep on going with all your might.

Keep on going to a land of hope
A land that lies where no one can see
And the land that is best
For you and for me.

Most of us can see better than we can hear. Janice made a profound impact on my life without even knowing it. She had found and expressed uniquely the peace that passes understanding.

Delight yourselves in the Lord, yes, find
your joy in him at all times. Have a
reputation for being reasonable, and never
forget the nearness of your Lord.
    Don't worry over anything whatever;
whenever you pray tell God every detail of
your needs in thankful prayer, and the
peace of God, which surpasses human

understanding, will keep constant guard over your hearts and minds as they rest in Christ Jesus.

I have learned to be content, whatever the circumstances may be.

—PHILIPPIANS 4:4-7, 12 (PHILLIPS)

Learning
from Children

*Let the little children come to me, and do
not hinder them, for the kingdom of God
belongs to such as these. I tell you the
truth, anyone who will not receive the
kingdom of God like a little child will
never enter it.* —MARK 10:14b, 15

*We try to make our children be more like
us instead of becoming more like them—
with the results that we pick up none of
their good traits and they pick up most of
our bad ones.* —SYDNEY HARRIS

We ARE CHALLENGED in more than one place in
Scripture to stay childlike. Not childish, but childlike. In fact, St.
Paul wrote, "When I was a child, I talked like a child, I thought

like a child, I reasoned like a child. When I became a man, I put childish ways behind me" (I Corinthians 13:11).

Some people cling to all of the worst attributes of childhood. They insist on staying selfish, unreasonable, helpless, and spoiled. But Jesus is encouraging us to stay childlike—wide-eyed, full of wonder, trusting, and humble.

"Therefore, whoever humbles himself like this child is the greatest in the kingdom of heaven" (Matthew 18:4). To be humble means not to make comparisons. Children have this kind of freedom. They insist, without knowing it, on just being themselves. They take life as it is. Head on, full blast, living to the hilt. They live in the present. They are not overwhelmed by worry or guilt. They take their significance for granted and want to respond to the world in a wide-open manner.

I heard two little boys talking and one said, "My dad can beat up your dad." To which the other little boy responded, "Big deal. So can my mom." I loved it!

A little boy once spent a lot of time and energy making a wonderful boat. It was blue and white. It had a little rudder and a magnificent sail that he had made from a sheet. The day finally arrived when he could take it down to the lake and watch it sail. It was a little windier than he had anticipated, but he thought, *That will just make it go faster.* He tied a string to the back of the boat so it wouldn't get away.

The wind caught the sail with an unexpected firmness. He was excited to see how fast it went. The string was going out of his hand at a rapid rate. The only problem was, he forgot to tie the string to his finger . . . and before he knew it, the string left his hand and the boat kept on going. He chased it out into the water, wading up to his waist, but he couldn't catch the little boat. He watched it sail off over the horizon. He was brokenhearted. All of his work was gone, and his very special boat was now lost.

For days he moped around the house, unable to be consoled. Then one afternoon, his mother asked him to get a loaf of bread at the grocery store. He gathered the change, put it into his pocket, and headed out for the store. Along the street he had to pass a pawnshop, and there in the window was his boat. His heart just about jumped out of his shirt.

He ran into the store and said, "Mister, mister, that's my boat! That's my boat you've got in the window. I'm here to get my boat."

The pawnshop owner looked down at him and said, "I'm sorry, son, but that's my boat now. I found it. If you want to get your boat back, you will have to pay me for it."

The little boy looked up and asked him, "How much do I have to pay you?"

To which the man replied, "Two dollars and fifty cents."

The little boy thought to himself, *Two hundred and fifty pennies. How will I ever get that much?* But he knew that no matter how long it took or how hard it would be, he would get his boat back. When he went back home, he told his mother what had happened. She offered him jobs around the house so he could earn ten cents here, fifteen cents there, and, for really big tasks, even a quarter. He also went out and asked the neighbors if he could do odd jobs for them to make money. He wanted to get his boat back as fast as he could.

Finally, after much hard work, the day arrived. He gathered his coins, put them into a can, and carried them carefully to the pawnshop. When the pawnbroker gave the little boy his boat, the child hugged it tightly to himself.

On the way out the door, the boy was overheard saying: "Little boat, you are twice mine. I made you, I lost you, and then I bought you back again."

What a powerful illustration of our relationship to the Lord. God has legitimate claim to our lives because we are twice His. He made us, He lost us, and then, through His Son, He bought us back again. Today as you struggle with your loneliness, remember all that God has done to make you His. He made you, He lost you, and He bought you back again.

One of the greatest dangers in loneliness is to focus on ourselves. Perhaps the worse thing that we can do is to get locked into self-pity. When our focus is on God and how much He has invested in us, we are free to get a new perspective on life.

A pastor friend sent me the following "essay on God" written by Danny Dunton, an eight-year-old southern Californian. Here is what he wrote.

One of God's main jobs is making people. He makes these to put in place of the ones that die, so there will be enough people to take care of things here on earth. He doesn't make grown-ups. Just kids. I think it's because they are smaller and easier to make. That way He doesn't have to take up His valuable time teaching them to talk and walk. He can just leave that up to moms and dads. I think it works out pretty good.

God's second most important job is listening to prayers. An awful lot of this goes on, as some people like pastors pray other times besides bedtime. . . . God sees everything, hears everything, and is everywhere, which keeps Him pretty busy. . . .

Jesus is God's Son. He used to do all the hard work, like walking on water and doing miracles and trying to teach people about God who didn't want to learn. They finally got tired of His preaching to them and they crucified Him. But He was good and kind like His Father, and He told His Father that they didn't know what they were doing and to forgive them, and God said OK. His Father appreciated everything He had done and all His hard work on earth, so He told

Him He didn't have to go out on the road anymore. He could stay in heaven. So He did. And now He helps His Father out by listening to prayers and seeing which things are important for God to take care of and which ones He can take care of Himself without having to bother God. You can pray anytime you want and they are sure to hear you because they've got it worked out so one of them is on duty all the time. . . .

➤ *NTS:*

Today remember that God is listening to the deepest yearnings in your heart. Remember that He is "on duty" all the time. Remember that He sees everything, hears everything, and is everywhere. Remember that He loves us . . . immensely. With a childlike simplicity, offer your prayers to God and really experience Him hearing you.

CHRIS SLAGLE AND I were driving in a car in West Virginia. As we came up behind a van, we saw kids in the van in front of us put a sign in the back window which said, "MAKE A FACE." We made the best faces that we possibly could. Their faces left the window for a few moments, then all of a sudden they came back with a sign with big, red letters saying, "THANK YOU."

We decided to join in the fun. We grabbed the biggest sheet of paper that we could find in the car and wrote in big, bold letters, "MAKE A PIG FACE." The kids in the back of the van laughed so hard that they steamed up the windows. Then they did one of the best impressions of a pig face that I've ever seen. We in turn flipped our piece of paper over and wrote out a big thank-you.

➳ *NTS:*

God loves to laugh. And He wants us to learn how to play as well as pray. Take a few minutes out today and make a pig face. In fact, go to the mirror in the bathroom and make the biggest pig face that you possibly can. When you have done that, look at the person in the mirror and say, "Thank you."

And then during the day don't forget to say thank you to God for His love, His laughter, and His presence.

CHILDREN'S PRAYERS are usually very simple and to the point. One day when my younger son, Josh, was little, he had been suffering from an earache. At bedtime, he and his mom decided to have a time of prayer. They decided that Mom would pray for Josh, and then Josh would pray for her. Pam prayed a simple, earnest prayer regarding Josh's earache.

A few moments later, Josh looked back at his mom and announced, "He said, 'YUP!'"

"What?" Pam asked.

"We asked Jesus to take the pain away, and Jesus came into my ear and took the fire away. He said, 'YUP.'"

Jesus is the divine YES. He is the affirmation of all life. Invite Him into your life today in newer and simpler ways.

> *But they that wait upon the Lord shall renew their strength. They shall mount up with wings like eagles; they shall run and not be weary; they shall walk and not faint.* —ISAIAH 40:31 (TLB)

ON THE WALL of my office is a huge photograph of an eagle flying majestically in front of a magnificent mountain range. I also have an eagle mug, an eagle knife, an eagle watch, and pictures and more pictures of eagles. I have a nearly life-sized wood carving of an eagle in flight that I purchased in the Philippines several years ago. I also have a hand-carved stone head of an eagle that is so lifelike that you almost have to touch it to see if it's real.

In the past two decades I've collected so many versions of

eagles that my wife has threatened to disown me if I bring home another. You might say I'm obsessed.

But one of my favorite eagles is also the simplest. Most people would overlook it. It's drawn on an old piece of cardboard in red, black, and yellow markers. An eagle, half standing and half in flight, stands atop some wiggly lines that could be mountains. The sun makes a bold appearance in the upper right-hand corner. And it says "I love you" boldly and beautifully, though the words aren't actually written anywhere on the cardboard. The misspelled title just above the eagle's head read "King fo the sky."

I don't know which of the boys drew it. It could have been either Josh or Zac—or maybe even both. They must have been very young—before love became complicated by age and knowledge. The love expressed on that old piece of cardboard is clear and uncluttered—something all too rare these days. Oh, my boys still love me, to be sure . . . but it's harder to find those simple, unadorned manifestations. They don't draw me pictures anymore.

On lonely days, I look at my eagle and remember that I am loved. I remember that I am Loved.

Children's stories sometimes communicate the most profound truths. In the well-known story *The Velveteen Rabbit* by Margery Williams, the Skin Horse has a special message for each of us in our loneliness.

"What is REAL?" asked the Rabbit one day, when they were lying side by side near the nursery fender, before Nana come to tidy the room. "Does it mean having things that buzz inside you and a stick-out handle?"

(How many of us think that the answer to our loneliness is in something fancy, something cosmetic, something that we do to our outside to make us more appealing?)

"Real isn't how you are made," said the Skin Horse. "It's a thing that happens to you. When a child loves you for a long, long time, not just to play with, but REALLY loves you, then you become Real."

"Does it hurt?" asked the Rabbit.

"Sometimes," said the Skin Horse, for he was always truthful. "When you are Real you don't mind being hurt."

(God's love is sometimes painful. Whereas the Valentine Day kind of love is pictured as a heart with an arrow through it, God's immense love for us is depicted by a heart with a cross going through it. It was painful for God to love us as much as He did. It will not necessarily be unpainful for Him to make us whole and real.)

"Does it happen all at once, like being wound up," he asked, "or bit by bit?"

(All of us would like to have our loneliness fixed instantly, but that is not the way life works.)

> *"It doesn't happen all at once," said the Skin Horse. "You become. It takes a long time. That's why it doesn't often happen to people who break easily, or have sharp edges, or who have to be carefully kept. Generally, by the time you are Real, most of your hair has been loved off, and your eyes drop out and you get loose in the joints and very shabby. But these things don't matter at all, because once you are Real you can't be ugly, except to people who don't understand."*[3]

So many of us in our loneliness try to become more attractive so that we will be more lovable. We think that that will somehow heal us, make us whole, make us real. The truth is that we need a Love that lasts for a long, long time from Someone who is not playing with us, but really loves us. So He heals us bit by bit. Sometimes our joints get loose and we may get very shabby, but these things don't matter at all, because once you are real you can never be ugly again, except to people who don't understand.

ะๅ *FROM MY JOURNAL:*
When our striving fails, He is a God who comes to find us—even when we can't find ourselves. All too often we think we have to change, be good, to grow in order to be loved. In truth we are loved in order to

*change and grow and be all the things that
God wants us to be.*

*I know that He really loves me, but I just
forgot for awhile.* —MARTHA J., AGE 41

O UR PASTOR TOLD a wonderful story about the power
and wisdom of children. It was a story about Johnny, a young boy
who had a terminal disease and not long to live. His disease made
it very difficult sometimes for him to understand classroom assign-
ments. During the Easter season, the children were supposed to
take an empty "Easter egg" (actually a L'eggs panty hose container)
and put something in it that reminded them of life and of Easter.

The day the eggs were turned in, the teacher opened each one
in turn and made a positive comment on what each child had put
inside. Observing that one egg was empty, she assumed that it was
Johnny's and that, as usual, he didn't understand the assignment.

When she finished, Johnny raised his hand and said, "But,
Teacher, you didn't share mine."

"I'm sorry, Johnny, but you didn't understand. You were to
bring something that means Easter to you, that represents life, and
put it into the egg."

"But Teacher," Johnny said, "Jesus' tomb was empty—and that is what life is really all about."

Johnny died a few weeks later, and in his casket his classmates placed twenty-seven empty eggs. They understood.

He is risen; He is risen; He is risen indeed. His empty tomb means our hearts can be full.

Who's Got Time?

W E N O L O N G E R savor life for what it is. We bolt down our life as if it were a hamburger patty getting cold on the edge of a shivering plate. We insatiably gulp down our incomplete and undigested experiences as fast as we can stuff them in—as if there were no tomorrow.

Each tired day covers us with another layer of insulation—the noise, the clutter, the crowds, the busyness—and our awareness grows so dim and superficial that nothing seems so lonely to us as our simple being.We no longer savor life for what it is. A miracle. An instant. A glimpse. A gift.

> *When we start being too impressed by the results of our work, we slowly come to the erroneous conviction that life is one large scoreboard where someone is listing the points to measure our worth. . . . In*

solitude we become aware that our worth is not the same as our usefulness. . . . It is in solitude that this inner freedom can grow. —HENRI NOUWEN

I HAVE HEARD IT SAID that "one of the ultimate forms of laziness is busyness!" As long as one is busy, busy, busy, he or she never has to face what is really important in life. We never have to find out who God really is. We simply follow the God we have underlined in the Bible—not the God who is, but the God we want Him to be. All we have to do is carefully ignore anything in Scripture that doesn't meet our specifications of God—and never spend time alone with Him. We can be busy at work, busy at home, and busy at church. All work equally well at helping us ignore God as He really is.

Solitude is a flower born of simplicity. It needs to be tended slowly and patiently. A quiet heart never comes easy, never in a hurry. Hearts like yours and mine can become completely numbed by too much busyness.

We read so much about the courage involved in heroic actions that we fail to realize that perhaps one of the most courageous things that one can do today is truly to "be still, and know that [He] is God" (Psalm 46:10).

➡ *NTS:*

If God speaks to us anywhere, He speaks to us in our daily lives. What are two or three details of your life that you can turn over to God today? Ask God for guidance in some specific act today.

What is your loneliness trying to say to you? Pascal's oft-quoted statement that within each of us is a God-shaped vacuum seems worth saying one more time. Is it possible that your loneliness is trying to remind you that there are some holes that only God can fill?

🐌 *FROM MY JOURNAL:*
Loneliness does not always come from emptiness. Sometimes it is because we are too full... full of ourselves. Full of activity. Full of distractions. Paradoxically, if I want to heal the loneliness in my life, I've got to get away... to be alone with God.

SOME YEARS AGO Summit ran a wilderness course for the national directors of a large Christian organization. The theme was to be "Solitude and Community." Our whole staff was excited and spent countless hours of preparation for the seven-day course.

A week and a half before the course, we were informed by the principal organizer that they had to cut the course to five days because they were so busy. We were disappointed, because "solitude and community" above all else take time, but we adjusted some of the activities and still figured out ways for them to get the time together that they needed.

Four days before the course, we were informed that the course had to be cut to three days in length—because they were so busy. Again adjustments were made—and again we rearranged space in between rock climbing and rappeling for the men to have time alone and time together.

The day before the course, we were told that since all these people were national directors of the organization, they were very important—and so busy—that we had to cut the course down to two days.

The men arrived the next day, and our staff set about trying to help them discover the depths and facets of community. The rock climbing was abbreviated; the rappeling was shortened; the hiking was taken out almost altogether. Rather than have them work together doing all the cooking and camping chores, which really builds community, we decided that it was much more "efficient" to have the staff do it for them.

In the middle of the second day, the director of the directors told us that we should probably cut day two "a little short" because some of their people had reminded him that they had many calls to make—they were very busy.

So we all returned to base camp, where I was told that I would have about four and a half hours to facilitate a discussion on solitude and community. I had prepared a sixty-four page notebook for each of the participants (originally planned to be discussed over a seven-day course). I knew that I wouldn't be able to cover the entire contents, but I thought that I could hit the highlights, point out where they could read further, and then facilitate a discussion on what the Body of Christ meant to them and what the essence of community was in their experience.

Just before we were to start, I was informed that we only had about forty-five minutes because they were "very busy." I started by sharing that community comes from the same root as the words for "communication" and "communion." The community of Christ is made, as in communion, from broken bread and crushed grapes. "As we communicate to each other in our brokenness, we begin to discover what true community is all about. . . ."

I looked around and noticed that no one was paying any attention to me. These men, very highly esteemed in their profession, had flown in from all over the country for this experience—but they were now intensely engrossed in their datebooks and calendars.

I paused, tried another angle. "Dietrich Bonhoeffer says that you don't build community, you accept it. In his book *Life Together* he says that countless Christian communities have broken down because they sprang from a wish dream, that people were more committed to their idea of community than to the reality of Christ in the world. Community is a divine reality, not—"

I looked around again. No one was paying attention. They were all very busy, now locked into their Daytimers. I paused. Waited. No response. Then I said quietly, "I realize that we have very little time left. I just want to tell you thanks for the impact you have made on my life."

The words "impact on my life" hit a cordial nerve in their corporate self. A few heads popped up.

"Seriously," I continued, "you have made an indelible impact on my life. In fact, I will never be the same."

It was like someone had just opened a window in the room. These men were world-changers. Now they were hearing that they had changed yet another life. Pride in their mission swelled. It filled the room.

"I will never forget what you have taught me. . . ." I continued.

A few of them were trying to figure out how they had made such a life-changing impact on me in such a short time—but then, they were world-changers. They were used to meaningful exchanges in a short amount of time. In fact, they had to keep getting better and better and better and faster and faster if they were going to change the whole world for Christ's sake.

I continued to tell them how they had touched my life. By now some were even nodding their heads—acknowledging that yet another lost soul had been touched by their light. I waited until all eyes were focused on me. It got very still. All their pens had been laid down, and in the last remaining minutes they were going to hear my praise for what they had accomplished—and in such a short amount of time. Yes, they were getting better.

"I will never forget what you have taught me. You have shown me in indelible fashion precisely who I never want to become as a Christian! Thank you."

There was a not-so-subtle gasping of breaths—not only from them but from some of our staff as well. Mouths dropped open. Eyes went glassy. They sat there in stunned silence. Even I was surprised at what I had said. I plunged ahead.

"I'm quite serious. I respect your work, but I never want to become so busy that I don't have time for my friends—and even God Himself. You all seem to believe that if you are not in Houston on Wednesday and in New York on Friday that the Kingdom is going to fall apart. I hate to tell you this—but it isn't. In some ways you are serving an impotent God—one who depends on your busyness. I'm sorry, but that's not the God I know."

No one had ever confronted them like this. They were ready to tar and feather me and ship me out on the first train until one man spoke up.

"Hold it. I think he really has something important to say to us—if we can stand to hear it. In fact, I admire his guts. Normally people are too afraid of us or in too much awe of us to challenge us. Perhaps he's right. We are too busy for each other and for taking ample time aside to listen to our God."

Our limited time together after that was, needless to say, challenging and profitable. We all tried our best to be open and let God say to us what we needed to hear. I was glad I had taken the risk—and in the long run, so were they.

➤ *NTS:*

Christ frequently asked people to do difficult things. To the paralytic He said, "Pick up your bed and walk." To Peter He said, "Drop your nets. Leave them behind and follow Me." He encourages us to love our enemies; to lose our lives in order to find them; to pick up our crosses daily and follow Him. His love is not a wimpy love. It is a "hard-nosed *agape.*"

What is He saying to you today? What areas of your life are not conformed to His image? He became like us so that we could become more like Him. Let God challenge you to the core. "But remember, the Christ you have to deal with is not a weak person outside you, but a tremendous power inside you" (II Corinthians 13:3, Phillips).

For a practical exercise, try going the next twenty-four hours without complaining. It is tougher than you think.

IN MY STERILE SEARCH for success, I have sometimes chosen to be effective rather than committed. I have chosen to be successful rather than merely being faithful. Sometimes my calendar is full, but my heart is empty. The Lord tries to fill my cup, but I poke a hole in it. Perforated trust.

Am I afraid to trust Him completely? Am I afraid to love others without knowing whether or not I'll be loved in return? I still don't understand His kind of love—a love which expects nothing.

I tend to calculate and define. Evaluate and measure. Make sure that everything is equal. I am an accountant rather than a disciple. It's hard to give with a closed fist, or receive with a calculator in your hand. My feelings go up and down more than the Dow Jones charts.

As Ian Thomas says, God doesn't ask us to be sensational—He simply asks us to be a miracle. A miracle is something that cannot be explained apart from Jesus Christ. He wants to borrow our humanity to communicate His truths to the world. He doesn't give us His strength, He is our strength.

A broken heart simply contains more room for love. In my own personal dark night of the soul, it felt like the vacuum within me was getting bigger and bigger. Then I realized that this "hollowness" was simply creating more room and more appetite for God. My cup of emptiness became a Cup for His Presence and His Love.

We must remain "empty" in our loneliness (that is, not trying to fill it with every possible distraction), or He cannot fill us.

And this love that He gives is pure gift. Therefore we must struggle through the mine field of our doubts to open our hearts to gratitude. Too many of us wait and wait for the perfect gift, and it never comes.

As Lewis Smedes says, "The perfect gift comes only now and then: most gifts are slightly flawed. But if we focus on the flaws, we quench the joy. People who demand perfection of gifts choke gratitude before it gets a chance to make them or anyone else glad."

Wouldn't It Be Wonderful?

  ❧ *FROM MY JOURNAL:*

Sometimes I worry about us. At the most critical time in history, we're sitting like pickles in a jar getting preserved—safe, careful, nice dead people. What would it be like knowing God without having our shirts tucked in, without having our shirts pressed?

We are all pretending to look good. Stiff, starched, impeccably careful, saved and safe. Like potato salad at a church picnic.

It is a sad truth that at times people have found the church to be a place for looking good rather than a place where struggles are shared and accepted. —DAVID NORTON

BRENNAN MANNING has written a captivating book called *The Ragamuffin Gospel* which, in his words, is news for the "bedraggled, beat-up, and burnt out." In it he talks about the immense, outrageous love of God. But he says at the same time we must give up our naive concept of a pastel-colored, patsy God who promises never to rain on our parade.

He tells a story of a pastor who did a Bible study on Genesis 22, where God commands Abraham to take his son, Isaac, out and offer him in sacrifice on Mount Moriah. After the group read the passage, the pastor gave some historical background on this period, including the prevalence of child sacrifice among the Canaanites. The group listened to what he said in awkward silence. Then the pastor said, "But what does this story mean to us?"

A middle-aged man spoke up. "I'll tell you what this story means to me. I've decided that my family and I are looking for another church."

The pastor was astonished. "Why?" he asked.

"Because," the man said, "when I look at that God, the God of Abraham, I feel I'm near a real God, not the sort of dignified, businesslike, Rotary Club God we chatter about here on Sunday mornings. Abraham's God could blow a man to bits, give and then take a child, ask for everything from a person, and then want more. I want to know that God."[4]

That is the God that I want to know, too. With all my heart and all my feelings. Many of us have learned to geld our feelings in order to fit in the church. We've become emotional eunuchs so as not to ripple the waters. Sometimes I've felt like Pinocchio—a little wooden boy who wants desperately to be real. But, I've been afraid that if I really expressed my true feelings, I wouldn't fit into the Kingdom.

Rather than risk the splendor of real feelings, we have chosen to reveal only those that are safe and sterilized. Those that are pretested and acceptable. We have chosen a "Christian reputation" over the risk of a genuine unpredictable relationship with Jesus Christ. Feelings are at the heart of our relationship to Christ—and to each other. When we forbid certain feelings, we risk the desolation and depression of loneliness.

The solace that comes from being accepted as we really are has eluded us. What an irony for an organization which is based on the unconditional love of the wounded Christ. We are understocked with people who feel real feelings and express them. If the passionate resurrected Christ truly lives within us, then shouldn't some of His feelings for a desperate world show through?

As Vance Havner said, "The great tragedy today is that the situation is desperate, but the saints are not." In a herd we travel the well-worn paths, afraid to risk the adventure of newness, timidly shying away from the unknown. The Bible is crammed with wilderness experiences—but we prefer to graze on fenced-in land. Without knowing it, we have denounced risky people as outlaws and openly forced them outside our boundaries with barbed-wire fences. And sometimes our sterile sanctuaries are shocking reminders of the power of unacceptance. Our young people sometimes rage against the restraint but eventually succumb—or else are gently encouraged to go elsewhere.

Are there no more frontiers for the church? Is there no wilderness? No wildness? Perhaps the freedom that Christ wanted to give us has been dammed up, detoured, and ultimately tamed. The twinkle in our eyes has been dulled by conformity. Our unpredictable childlikeness has been concealed behind more acceptable formality. These feelings that flow with abundance in our youth have faded even more than our bodies. They are now stiff, careful, cautious, proper. We don't need "fasten your seat belts" signs in our pews because we no longer fly. We're like a group of geese attending meetings every Sunday where we talk passionately about flying—and then get up and walk home!

It is infrequent if not impossible to hear of a church that could be described as "rowdy with the love of God." It is getting more and more costly to feel the anger, the compassion, and the loneliness that Jesus did. Those who are tipsy with the love of God are encouraged to be a little more antiseptic.

The Jesus I know leaks into the difficult places and joyfully overflows into problem places and people. He erupts into the geography of need. Steals into the bruised crevices of hurt—the black and blue areas of pain. He is not safe. And when He fully invades a person by invitation, literally anything can happen. He doesn't come in to rearrange the furniture; He is into reconstruction. He doesn't repair; He recreates. He is not so interested in making us "religious" as in making us whole "in a way that we would never even dare ask or imagine." He was considered dangerous to public safety when He walked upon this earth. Today this same Jesus is seeking men and women who will allow Him to be Himself—in all His fullness and unpredictability.

As my good friend Jim Wilson says: "If you really understand that salvation calls us to a passionate interaction with a hurting world, then perhaps instead of being bored to tears, you would be moved to them."

➡ *NTS:*

> Many of us can fall into the trap of just going
> through the motions. I know that I certainly can.
> My prayers get a little more anemic. I become a
> little more concerned with my agenda than with
> God's.

To show the splendor of the newborn Savior in the church Christmas pageant, an electric light bulb was hidden in the manger. All the stage lights were to be turned off so only the brightness of the manger could be seen, but the boy who controlled the lights got confused, and suddenly all the lights went out. It was a fairly tense moment broken by a little shepherd's loud whisper, "Hey, you just switched off Jesus!"

I switch off Jesus much more than I am willing to admit. If you and I were to switch Jesus back on in our lives, what would He be saying to us? Prayer is listening to Him, not just telling Him what you need. In fact, it's finding out what He needs and wants from you, where He can use you to fill a need or create a bridge where there is a gap of loneliness.

But you say, "I'm lonely, too. Why doesn't someone come to me?" It is interesting that the passage in Isaiah doesn't say "Here I am, find me," nor does it say "fill my needs." The Scriptures are clear. The correct response is, "Here I am, send me" (Isaiah 6:8).

Take the next tiny step. Psalm 18:28 (KJV) says, "The Lord my God will enlighten my darkness." As He does so, be willing to take the steps that He has prepared for you. Allow God to direct you and to be fully Himself in your life.

ISN'T IT A GREAT IRONY that when the Son of God actually visited us on earth, one of the chief complaints against Him was that He wasn't religious enough? Almost a hundred years ago, Charles Sheldon wrote a book called *In His Steps*. In it a pastor challenges his people to live by the devastatingly simple question, "What would Jesus do?" In doing so they turn a whole town upside down with the incredible love of Christ.

The Book of Acts likewise describes a group of men and women who were turned inside out and upside down. They changed the world for Jesus Christ. The impact of their simple undeviating commitment is still affecting the world.

We have a kingdom of upside-down values and a King who didn't conform. The irony is that His followers spend most of their time and energy trying to turn things right side up to make them more respectable and acceptable. We encourage people to be more careful and sensible. We would turn them right side up and teach them to be proper believers. A pastor, in a moment of great but painful insight, once said, "Isn't it curious that wherever St. Paul went there was a riot . . . but wherever I go there is a tea party?"

Wouldn't it be wonderful if, just for a day or two, our churches were described as :

Risky

Revolutionary

Dangerous

Ruthlessly honest and open

Unconditionally loving

Radical

Rowdy

Not quite off the page, but certainly in the margin

Challenging

Adventurous

Unpredictable

Curious

Life-changing

Stirred up

Paradoxical

A place that will accept you just as you are

Contagious

Flat out crazy in love with God

Digging into reality at its deepest level

People who have encountered an incandescent living God

People who are so outrageously committed that they are at a point of no return

People who will really stop and listen to your pain

People who are interested in individuals and not in crowds

People who make lots of mistakes because they take new risks

People who relish each day
People made noble by the presence of God
People who realize that God doesn't love them because they're
    good, but because they are sinners
People who would take you home like Zacchaeus if you needed it
People who don't want to imitate anyone except Christ Himself
People who are not sure what they will say and do next
People who are insatiably curious—who don't have all the
    answers
People who are willing to share their success and failures
People who are the greatest encouragers in the world
People who are free to be themselves and even admit their doubts
People who fly without wings
People who pray unceasingly
People who laugh, cry, and feel all their feelings
People who are really poor in spirit—so they have nothing to lose
    and everything to gain
People who don't justify themselves
People who are infectiously joyous and seek to give their lives
    away
People who are willing to be fools for Christ's sake

Wouldn't it be fun if, just for a few Sundays,
People raced each other to the front pews so they could respond
    with more excitement
The bulletins were blank—to be filled in by the Holy Spirit
We had to sit close together and maybe even in each other's laps
    because there were so many people at church
We ruffled each other's hair at the beginning of the service just so
    we wouldn't take each other too seriously
We laughed until tears came down our cheeks
We honestly shared with each other how much we are hurting

*We stamped our feet and clapped our hands out of sheer
  uncontrollable enthusiasm*
*We got so mixed up that we had to pray spontaneously from our
  hearts*
We united the spirit of God within us and among us
We met five people we didn't know before
We sang "Don't Fence Me In"
We didn't wear ties or tuck our shirts in
*We took off our watches and encouraged the pastor to just
  "preach until the Holy Spirit was done speaking"*
We truly "rested" in Christ

Fortunately, I know many churches with this kind of spirit, and I'm grateful. I've been invited to speak at churches that are electric with the presence of Christ, and whose love is absolutely contagious. These are people who face life at point blank, yet radiate a joy which is inextinguishable.

AGAIN AND AGAIN, we must remind ourselves that real life is messy, untidy, not purified, inconsistent, full of surprises and unexpected detours—for we are following One who is notoriously unpredictable.

The next time you see geese flying south for the winter in a V-formation, you might be interested in knowing what science has discovered about why they fly that way. There are four things that geese have to teach us.

One, they rotate their leadership. When the lead goose gets

tired, he rotates back in the wing and another goose flies point. (I'm sure one of the reasons leaders get lonely is because they are expected to stay in front all the time and they just plain wear out.)

The second thing that they do is to create an upward air current for one another. As each bird flaps its wings, it creates an uplift for the bird immediately following. Then, by flying in a V-formation, the whole flock gets seventy-one percent greater flying range than if each bird flew on its own. (Another reason for loneliness is that so many of us are all heading in our own directions rather than seeking to mobilize with each other in the same direction.)

Third, when a goose gets sick or is wounded by a shot or falls out, two geese fall out of formation and follow him down to help and protect him. They stay with him until he can fly again. (If people knew we would stand by them like that in the church, they would push down the walls to get in.)

Finally, it's the geese in the back who honk, letting the leaders know that they're following and all is well. (I am sure, too, that if people thought we would be constantly honking encouragement to them, our churches would have standing room only.)

When was the last time you stopped to encourage the pastor or one of the leaders in your church? Gave a honk of encouragement to a hurting or lonely person in your church? When we are focused together in a cooperative way in what God's call is, we are able to save much time and energy.

➡ *NTS:*

Write your own NTS. Do you know someone who could use a "honk" of encouragement today?

Letting Go

It's easy to change. It's easier not to.

*Not everything can be changed, but
nothing can be changed until it is faced.*
—JAMES BALDWIN

I AM NOT A THEOLOGIAN. I am not a scholar. I am just a writer. I cannot tell you how things should be; I can only tell you how I feel and what I have experienced. Although sometimes overwhelmed by confusion, I remain hopeful. Although sometimes overcome by loneliness, I still believe. I not only don't have all the answers, I'm sometimes not even sure I'm asking the right questions. Life is more complicated than I ever imagined. God's presence has brought peace, not certainty.

As I set out to write this book, I began reading, researching, finding out everything I could on the subject of loneliness. Countless hours later, it dawned on me that I must also look into the labyrinth of my own heart, which has volumes of memories of loneliness. Like yours, my heart is a library of loneliness, longing to be read, but most people come only to browse. All too often the real feelings go back on the shelf.

The loneliness talked about in these pages is not theoretical. In the laboratory of my own brokenness, I have sought to develop a theology that works. I don't believe that we have to go through our entire lives desperately lonely—but overcoming loneliness does require a willingness to change.

The Serenity Prayer ("God grant me the serenity to accept the things I cannot change, the courage to change the things I can, and the wisdom to know the difference") has been around so long that we overlook its timeless wisdom and insight. Recently I came across a variation on this prayer:

"God grant me the serenity to accept the person I cannot change, the courage to change the person I can, and the wisdom to know that I am that person." In truth, the only person we can ever change is ourselves.

> *I said I found peace. I didn't say that I was not lonely.* —ELISABETH ELLIOT

Most of us want to be fixed, made okay, free from pain and loneliness. We want to be protected from the wounds of everyday living.

God is not going to take all the loneliness away and patch every hole in our lives. He is just going to give it meaning and purpose. He doesn't promise to fix us—just make us whole and holy. St. Paul said, in the end of the letter to the Galatians, "Let no one interfere with me after this. I carry on my scarred body the marks of Jesus" (6:17, Phillips).

We still don't understand the Gospel story (perhaps we don't want to). When God raised Jesus from the dead, the imprint of the nails could still be seen. Why didn't God fix Him up? Why did He leave the scars? Can it be that the Gospel words are saying to us in our waiting, "You will not see Jesus Christ unless you see His wounds"? Somehow we must understand that the resurrected Christ is the wounded Christ. Living, but never "fixed up." Not bound by death, yet scarred for eternity.

The deaf have a sign for Jesus. The middle finger of each hand is placed in the palm of the other. Jesus, the one with wounded hands.

We must find our wholeness in the midst of our woundedness. We must find peace in the midst of our loneliness. We cannot wait for the scars to go away.

The Bible is a book about battles won and lost—and there are always scars. It has been said that when you get to heaven, God will not measure you for your diplomas or degrees or medals, but for your scars.

Any idiot can face a crisis. It's the day-to-day living that wears you out.
—Anton Chekov

WE LIKE TO TAKE LIFE in leaps and bounds. We like to make sure that everything is safe. But we find out that life is indefinite, that it is filled with a delicious ambiguity.

Life is a daily thing. By that I mean that no matter how we like to break up life to ease the burden, it still keeps falling into a day-to-day pattern. We have invented weeks, months, and years, but we can't live them. They only work in your Daytimer for scheduling. When it comes to actually living life, it's a daily sort of thing. We can only do it one day at a time, and it can never be "fixed." There will always be some heartache.

This is a lesson that I never seem to learn. I am always worrying about something that will happen next Wednesday or feeling bad about something that occurred last Friday. Perhaps that's because today is never easy.

Come to me . . . and I will give you rest.
—Jesus

LIVING IN CHRONIC PAIN leaves one ragged physically and emotionally. I haven't slept through a whole night in sixteen years. I wake up tired. I'm tired at breakfast. I'm tired at lunch.

I'm tired at dinner. I'm tired at work. I'm tired at home. I'm tired at play. Perhaps the worse thing about chronic pain is the chronic fatigue.

While traveling last summer, our family stopped at a lake for a picnic. The boys and I decided to go for a swim. After a short period of time, Zac and Josh went back to get more lunch. I decided just to float on my back. I completely relaxed . . . let go . . . let the water hold me. I was at total peace. I let go of the pain. It seemed like I was "resting" in the water. The immensity of the lake held me up.

I thought of Jesus' words, "Come to me . . . and I will give you rest" (Matthew 11:28). It is interesting to note that He didn't say, "Do this and it will give you rest" or "Don't do this, and that will give you rest." He said, "Come to me . . . and I will give you rest." It is an intimate relationship He offers.

We live in perhaps the most stressful period in human history. Most of us spend a good deal of time being tense, agitated, uptight, strained. Our jaws hurt. Our eyes hurt. Our joints hurt. In the midst of this, Jesus doesn't promise to make the problems go away. He doesn't say there will be no more stress or fatigue. He just says that in the middle of all of this we can know and experience rest. It's like having a refuge in the midst of all the craziness, a retreat center where we can go when life is just too much. It's peace amidst the storm. The eye in the middle of the hurricane. A place of stillness amidst the stress. An oasis. Hope amidst the confusion.

I had to learn how to float. My body was always capable of doing it, but I had to learn how to trust the water. Once I learned it was easy, and the more I did it, the easier it got. My confidence grew with experience.

Living in Christ is like that. The more I do it—the more I really let go—the easier it gets. My confidence grows with experience. I can catch my breath, let go. As I experienced in the lake, that which surrounds me does the work. I can just rest. I know that it will hold me because I have tested it.

The Bible says that this place we seek is a Person, that the peace that we look for is a presence rather than a principle. The simple truth is that we were made for God and therefore will never truly find rest anywhere else. This is a stubborn, profound, simple fact. Once we accept it with gratitude, we can return it with joy. From then on, alone doesn't have to mean lonely.

Isn't it interesting that Jesus says "Come to Me"? Personally, if I had a choice (and I do) I would rather trust a person than a principle. I'd rather trust a reality than a rule. I'd rather trust a living truth than a theory.

One of the greatest joys in my life is just being with my sons.

Zac is at the age where he is into cars, music, and girls (not necessarily in that order). Josh is at the age where basketball is the most important thing in his life (but he is beginning to discover girls). Both have a contagious sense of humor, and it's a joy just to be with them—we don't have to have an agenda.

Likewise our Father just wants to be with us, to spend time with us. Resting in God is just a matter of being with the Father. Sometimes we are called just to relax and do nothing. Just let go. Rest in Him and let go. We don't have to have an agenda.

As children bring their broken toys
with tears for us to mend,
I brought my broken dreams to God,
because He was my friend.
But then, instead of leaving Him
in peace, to work alone,
I hung around and tried to help,
with ways that were my own.
At last I snatched them back and cried,
"How can You be so slow?"
"My child," He said,
"What could I do?
You never did let go."

➤ *NTS:*

Are you "resting" in Christ? Have you truly come to that place where you can let go? Jesus says, "As the Father has loved Me, so have I loved you. Now remain in my love" (John 15:9).

If you live near a lake, try floating for a few minutes in the immensity of the lake on a warm, sunny day. Be as still as possible and imagine the hugeness of the lake holding you up. Try to translate that experience into your relationship with Christ.

In what areas of your life are you straining most? What is an NTS that you could take in this area?

I FEEL MOST INTENSELY LONELY when I try to fix the past or control the future. My mind wanders backwards to people and incidents which have caused someone pain . . . mistakes I have made or words that have hurt me. I review these in the movie of my mind, going over and over and over them. I wallow in guilt or anger, magnifying the events to justify the intensity of my feelings.

At other times I fearfully look forward. Anxious about something that might happen, I try to manipulate people or circumstances so as to cushion the potential pain. I maneuver my life to avoid a situation that may not even occur. I anticipate a hurtful situation that was never intended. And I draw myself into the very situation I was trying to avoid.

How strange we human beings are. We avoid what is, focusing instead on what might have been or what could be . . . condemning ourselves to a deeper experience of loneliness. We have isolated ourselves not only from people, but from understanding.

Where loneliness can be experienced in the past and the future as well, God, our only hope for healing, can be experienced in the present tense alone. His name is "I AM!"

> *What I want from you is your true thanks;*
> *I want your promises fulfilled. I want you*
> *to trust me in your times of trouble, so I*
> *can rescue you, and you can give me glory.*
>
> —PSALM 50:14, 15 (TLB)

I HAD A HIGH SCHOOL TEACHER who, when he wanted to be heard, would lower his voice. As the din in the room would get louder and louder, he would lower his voice almost to a whisper. When he did that, the entire class began to focus intently upon him, quieting down to a hush so they could hear him in his whispering voice.

God wants to speak to us. Sometimes He shouts to us through difficult circumstances; more often than we realize, He is whispering to us in our daily lives.

In I Kings 18-19 there is a story of God's whisper. It is the story of Elijah, who openly challenged the prophets of Baal to come up on Mt. Carmel for what ended up as the Bible's biggest barbecue. The confrontation demanded utmost confidence from Elijah—which he had. He boldly challenged all four hundred and fifty prophets to see whose God was real.

You know the outcome. The prophets of Baal pleaded with their gods, but "there was no voice and no one answered." Their gods had neither voice nor power. The prophets limped in defeat about the altar which they had made. Elijah mocked them and then prepared to demonstrate the power of the God of Israel.

He repaired the altar, which was in ruins. On the stones he arranged the wood. He cut the bull into pieces and laid it on the wood. Then he upped the ante by filling twelve large jars with water and pouring it over the wood. The water ran down the altar and even filled the trench. It was obvious that God would have to provide more than a little spark.

When the fire of the Lord fell, it burned up the sacrifice, the wood, the stones, and the soil, and even licked up the water in the trench. The people fell prostrate and cried, "The Lord, He is God.

The Lord, He is God." It was the most stunning success of Elijah's career.

But then circumstances changed, and Elijah's confidence waned. King Ahab's wife, Jezebel, came after Elijah with a vengeance. The prophet tried hiding from her and finally said, "I have had enough, Lord. Take my life." He felt terribly alone and afraid. "I am the only one left, and now they are trying to kill me, too."

He invoked God, and the answer came.

The Lord said, "Go out and stand on the mountain in the presence of the Lord, for the Lord is about to pass by." Then a great and powerful wind tore the mountains apart and shattered the rocks before the Lord, but the Lord was not in the wind. After the wind there was an earthquake, but the Lord was not in the earthquake. After the earthquake came a fire, but the Lord was not in the fire. And after the fire came a gentle whisper. —I KINGS 9:11,12

That was how God chose to speak to Elijah.

W E HAVE ALLOWED ourselves to be intoxicated by bigness. We sometimes anticipate that God can only speak to us through a spectacular event. We fail to realize that most of God's miracles are small, and that He often still chooses to speak to us in a still, small voice.

What is God simply trying to say to you these days? Perhaps He is saying, "Slow down." Perhaps He is reminding you that "to obey is better than sacrifice" (I Samuel 15:22). Perhaps He is gently trying to encourage you with His persistent love. Perhaps He is hoping that you will recall the extent of His forgiveness. Perhaps He is whispering to you in your loneliness—and it is an invitation to a deeper experience with Him.

My high school teacher realized that he couldn't get heard by yelling. God is trying to speak to you. Hush. Be still. Listen to Him in the quietness of your own heart. He says, "Be still and know that I am God" (Psalm 46:10a).

➡ *NTS:*

In your experience, how does God speak most clearly to you? Maybe it's while you're reading Scripture. Maybe it's in those quiet moments you have in your car on the way to work. God can speak to us anytime, anyplace. We don't have to be stopped altogether, but we do have to have a quiet, attentive, and eager heart.

Prayer is one of the most mysterious and powerful facets of our Christian walk—and perhaps the most critical. Without prayer our Christian life unravels. Prayer is the key, the core, the essence, the glue. A Christian without prayer is like a body without a heart. It's like a car without an engine. It might look great, but it has no power and is certainly not going anywhere.

What is your NTS? Do you pray by yourself or with others? Do you pray through Scripture or while taking a walk? Remember, listening is perhaps the most important part of prayer.

IT HAS BEEN SAID that a bore is someone who talks when you want him to listen. When I heard that, it dawned on me that much of our loneliness stems not from an absence of voices around us, but from an absence of listening to the voices. Listening and love are almost synonymous. One of the best ways to show God's love is by listening. Yet we live in a world where all of us are trying to impress each other with the quality of our words.

In the early '70s we had an assistant instructor in Summit who absolutely befuddled me until I learned her secret. Marcie was not gifted in mountaineering skills. She couldn't climb that well. She couldn't read a map that well and frequently got lost. She had a hard time remembering how to tie some of the knots. And when it came to the technical side of mountaineering she usually went blank. "What are these little things called again that you use for anchors?" "Could you show me one more time how to set up a belay?" "O yeah, I guess I did get those a little confused."

Her pack always looked like it had been packed on the run—cups dangling, bandanas blowing in the wind, extra gear tied to the outside straps. She wasn't very fast or very strong. And yet when the senior instructors set out to choose assistant instructors they were always fighting over who got Marcie. "I get dibs on Marcie this trip!" "You had her last time."

Marcie had a winsome and contagious smile. She was a joy to be with. But was that it? Was that why everyone wanted her in their group?

The joy was part of it. Joy is much stronger than any of us think. It is far more pervasive and life-changing that we can imagine, but that wasn't the only reason. What we finally discovered (and what impacted us all in a powerful way) was that Marcie was a profound listener. Whenever Marcie was on a course, lives were changed dramatically because she took time to listen. As people began to notice and watch her, they realized that Marcie's great gift to the course was her ability, and desire, to listen to people.

When people were waiting for snow school, you'd look over

and there was Marcie listening. As people were fixing dinner, there was Marcie listening. Frequently as you were snuggling down into the sleeping bag, you'd look over and realize there were some people still around the camp fire. And there right in the middle was Marcie—doing the most important thing we can ever do for people. She was listening.

It seemed as though no matter what happened on a course—the bears stole your food, you got lost for 72 hours, it rained on the day you were supposed to rockclimb, it snowed on you during solo, you dropped your favorite fishing pole into the lake—no matter what happened, if Marcie was there, it was always a good course. In fact, it usually was considered "great."

I was looking back through some old Summit pictures recently, fondly remembering my many years in the wilderness. I came across a number of photos of Marcie. You guessed it. In every picture we caught her listening.

If someone were to take a snapshot of you right now, would they catch you listening?

Reaching Out

It had never dawned on him that the
vitally important thing was to drop his
ego. . . . There is nothing the ego will not
seize upon to inflate itself. . . . That is why
mature Christian prayer leads us . . .
through loneliness and aridity, which
buries egoism and leads us out of ourselves
to experience God. —BRENNAN MANNING

IT WAS A BRILLIANT DAY. The week of instructor training had been intense and jammed with fun. The instructors broke up into small teams to practice their skills on long climbs. Three of us were going to climb The Toad—a gigantic, thousand-foot rockface east of camp. It could be seen from miles around and got its name from its toadlike appearance at sunset.

The climb would take us four to five hours. I was to be the

lead climber for our team, which consisted of two of our women staff and me. Sherril and Sandy were both strong climbers, so I knew it would be an exciting day.

We gathered at the bottom of the climb, prayed together, and then began to go over the gear. We would be roped together the entire climb. We checked the slings, the carabiners, the chocks, the harnesses, and every piece of equipment to insure safety. Just before I was to start, I pulled off an eagle necklace that I was wearing, saying, "I think I'll leave my eagle behind." Neither Sherril nor Sandy was watching me as I unhooked it, but I knew they heard my words. I tucked the eagle into a small pack that was staying.

The first pitch was a long, clean face without many places for protection. I always feel better when I can finally anchor in at the top. I belayed them up to where I was standing, a place large enough for all three of us to stand.

"You are really amazing," they said. The comment took me by surprise, because the first pitch, though barren of protection, was not that difficult a climb.

Throughout the day more comments were made. "You're so mature." "You're so spiritual." "You're so wonderful."

By the time we got to the top of the climb, it was late in the day. Again I was told how splendid I was. By now I was thoroughly confused and had to ask, "Will one of you please tell me why I'm so pickin' wonderful today?"

"We were so impressed," one of them informed me, "when you said at the beginning of the climb that you were going to leave your ego behind."

When I informed them that it was my "eagle" I'd left behind, and not my ego, they both roared with laughter—and abruptly took me down off the temporary spiritual pedestal that they had put me on.

Since that day I have thought on several occasions about the profundity of what they thought they had heard. Wouldn't we all be much better off most days if we "left our egos behind"?

Perhaps one of the main reasons we fall into loneliness and despair is that we are so preoccupied with ourselves, so invested in our own egos. We're so concerned with how we are doing that we can't seem to get a clear focus on what God is doing in us and around us.

Thomas Merton says, "When humility delivers a man from attachment to his own works and his own reputation, he discovers that true joy is only possible when we have completely forgotten ourselves. And it is only when we pay no more attention to our own life and our own reputation and our own excellence that we are at last completely free to serve God for His sake alone."

I'm reminded of a conversation between a little girl and her mother as they walked out of church. The mother asked her how she liked church that day. The girl replied that she thought it was good, but that she was a little confused.

"The pastor said that God was bigger than we are. Is that true?" she asked.

The mother responded that it was indeed true.

"He also said that God lives inside of us. Is that true, Mommy?"

Again the mother replied, "Yes."

"Well, then," said the girl, "if God is bigger than us, and if He lives inside of us, then shouldn't some of Him show through?"

➡ *NTS:*

Is God showing through in your life these days? What could you do to help people see the living Christ in you? Perhaps you could reach out to someone less fortunate than you. Will Rogers once said, "You can't throw a stone in any direction without finding someone in more need than you."

You really can't think of anything to do? Ask your church where there is a need you can fill. Perhaps you could visit the elderly or maybe even mow their lawns. Perhaps you could reach out to some of those lonely people in your church or organization. Maybe you could phone someone who is down or write a note of thanks to someone who needs encouragement. God doesn't ask us to take giant steps. He just asks us to take the next tiny step. When we take that step, His love shows through.

Joy always dies for people who can be grateful only for perfect gifts.
—LEWIS SMEDES

IF YOU ARE A PERFECTIONIST, you are just setting yourself up for loneliness. Looking for the "perfect mate," for example, leads into never finding anyone who can live up to your image. Likewise, to be perfectionists about ourselves leads to a desperate kind of loneliness, because we can never accept ourselves just as we are or believe that anyone else could accept us either.

For years I had a sign on the back of my office door that I read before I went out to teach classes. It said *Nihil Expecta*, which is Latin for "expect nothing." The more we expect from others and from ourselves, the greater our disappointment, resentment, and loneliness. I believe in goal setting, but when we set goals for our feelings we run into trouble.

A dear friend once said to me that the best thing we can do is to wake up each morning and say to God, "I expect nothing, O Lord" . . . and thus everything that happens is a gift.

> *Whatever a man sows, that he will also reap.* —GALATIANS 6:7

> *Hope, like faith, is nothing if it is not courageous.* —THORNTON WILDER

THE WHOLE IDEA is that if you sow sparingly, you will also reap sparingly. If you are simply waiting for everybody else to love you, that's exactly what you will find in return—everybody waiting for you to love them.

Mirrors and windows are both made of glass, but they serve two distinctly different purposes. A window allows you to see out, to see the world, to see others, to get a perspective on life. A mirror focuses on your preoccupation with yourself. What we have got to do with our loneliness is to change our mirrors to windows.

   FROM MY JOURNAL:
We are lonely because God Himself can't give us what we think we want. We must remember that He wants to give us far more than we can ask or even want to receive.

I once heard a speaker say that three of the biggest handicaps in life are beauty, success, and intelligence. We are all handicapped in some way: some by cerebral palsy, some by beauty, some by polio, some by rigid expectations, some by muscular dystrophy, some by intelligence, some by lack of education, some by lack of humanity. If I understood what he was saying, one can be handicapped by beauty in that it makes a person self-conscious, always wondering what people think and thus imprisoning the self and disabling the soul from the freedom to grow and to move.

Both joy and depth of character come from reaching out to others. Too much intelligence, beauty, or success can hurt us by turning us inward, so that we are forever focusing on our own wrinkled and puny soul.

The causes of loneliness are legion, but most revolve around our extreme concern for ourselves. Our ferocious hunger for more. Our commitment to the false belief that enough is never enough.

Our scandalous neglect of the loving presence of God.

I know a lady who sits and sulks in her loneliness. God has given her her share of gifts, but in her refusal to give them away she is unable to experience them and to grow. So selfish and preoccupied is she that she eventually gets lost in her own imprisoned soul. By her own choice she has placed prison bars between herself and others—and then she points, blames, and pleads.

It has been said that no growth can occur until blaming ceases. Perhaps that is true of our loneliness as well. As we cast our blame on others for their apparent lack of love, the ache will only grow deeper.

Some of us are looking so hard for the answer that we can't see the many gifts that surround us. Seeking so hard that we never take time to find.

It is difficult to receive when your fists are clenched.

It is impossible to embrace when your arms are crossed.

It is difficult to see when your eyes are closed.

It is hard to discover when your mind is made up.

And a heart that has sealed itself off from giving has unknowingly sealed itself off from the ability to receive love.

We have allowed ourselves to become intoxicated by the big-screen images, so much so that our starving hearts have become impenetrable to the little daily acts of love by those who are nearest to us. For example, I sometimes wait impatiently for Pam and my boys to say "I love you" in a way that I think will fix me forever—and so I miss entirely the incredibly loving gestures that blossom forth every day. Love is rarely grandiose and majestic—it is usually gentle, quiet, and subtle.

Have you heard this parable that illustrates the difference between heaven and hell? In both situations, people are sitting at a banquet table overflowing with bounteous food. In both scenarios, everyone seated at the table has splints strapped to their arms that cannot be removed.

Obviously it wouldn't be possible to feed yourself if you couldn't bend your arms. In hell everyone is starving to death at the banquet table. But in heaven the banquet guests have discovered that, since their arms are strapped, each person can only feed the person across the table. Each feeds another, and all receive all they need.

Love is a celebration of giving as well as receiving. So many of us are starved for affection that can only be received if we give ourselves away. As we reach out in our brokenness, our arms splinted so that we cannot feed ourselves, we will be given what we need in return.

Our devious media have convinced us that love is something that happens to us; thus we are constantly trying to make ourselves appear more lovable. We fix and fuss. We make up and make over. We work our way up the ladder and we work out. We take vitamins and rub lotions all over our bodies. We primp and perfume. We starch and stretch. We do plastic surgery and practice plastic sentences. We try new hairdos, new clothes, and new ideas. We try on new perspectives and new preferences. Eventually we strangle ourselves in our attempts to be more attractive, to create a more powerful magnet for the love and attention that we so desperately desire. We wait and wait for that perfect person who will come along, sweep us off our feet, and make everything all right . . . while countless opportunities slip by us unnoticed.

The handicap in beauty, intelligence, or success lies in the fact that we spend our whole lives trying to make ourselves lovable rather than being committed to loving. When love finally comes, we devour it so ferociously that we can't even taste it or experience it.

There must be a better way. I think there is. In I John the writer says, "We love because [God] first loved us" (4:19). I think that means that there is a more healthy sequence for our seeking of love and attention.

God loves (and we must let Him do so lavishly).

Therefore, we are set free (to love Him, to love others, and to love ourselves).

And then, because love is like a boomerang, the wholeness of love we seek can come to us (and because we have already been filled to some extent by God's love, enough will be enough).

➳ *NTS:*

I heard a story about how actress Joan Blondell used to pull herself out of the dumps. She said, "I set the timer for six and a half minutes to be lonely and twenty-two minutes to feel sorry for myself. Then when the bell rings I take a shower, go for a walk or a swim, or I cook something and think about something else."

Isn't that great? Got a timer? Do something different today. Anything. Drive to work a different way. Play some different music. Rearrange your furniture. It won't cost you anything but a little creativity.

Stop feeling sorry for yourself. Jog in triangles. Throw a party. Make a three-minute commitment to joy. Sometime later in the day choose another three minutes and then another. Do something you've never done before. Wear different color socks. Put on the brightest shirt or sweater that you have—backwards. Assign names to all the potatoes in a ten-pound bag and see how many of them you can remember tomorrow. Play connect the dots with the freckles on your face.

I once heard Mike Warnke say, "Joy is when you are in your deepest valley and you can still believe for the mountaintop. Joy is when you are at your darkest point and you can still believe in the light. Joy is when you are confused 'beyond the point of recognition' but you still know that God is in control and that the Holy Spirit has a special plan for your life."

Thank God for five things. Right now. This instant. Rededicate your life to Him. And keep inching along with those next tiny steps.

So whatever you wish that men would do to you, do so to them. —MATTHEW 7:12

It is important to stress that every human being is called upon to be a healer. Although there are many professions asking for special long and arduous training, we can never leave the task of healing to the specialists. We are all healers who can reach out. —HENRI NOUWEN

I ALWAYS LOOK FORWARD to Ken's smile and friendly handshake. No matter how tough my day has been, he makes it seem as though the world is a friendly place. Ken works at the Soup Exchange, a newly opened soup-and-salad restaurant of high quality—perhaps my favorite place to eat in the town of San Dimas. Part of that is because of Ken's friendliness. I've watched him in his interactions with "clients," as he calls them. He is friendly, open, caring, and easy to talk to.

I mentioned that to him one night. "You are really good at what you do, Ken."

He said, "Maybe it's because of my basic loneliness. I need to reach out to people. I like the exchanges, the energy it produces. I find that when I reach out to other people, they reach back to me. In a sense, my own loneliness is a gift. It encourages me to keep reaching out to others."

The principle is as solid as the law of gravity. When I reach out to people, they in turn reach out to me. Jesus said it this way: "Do to others what you would have them do to you" (Matthew 7:12). This, He said, is the teaching of the law of Moses in a nutshell.

Perhaps one of the strongest reasons that people are so lonely is because they refuse to reach out themselves. They are constantly waiting for the world to reach out to them. Many falsely believe that their loneliness is caused by circumstances beyond their control. They somehow believe that the remedy is out of their hands, that it is the responsibility of other people or God. So they keep waiting for others to make friendly overtures to them.

Waiting for the world to come to you is a lonely place. I admit that it takes a lot of courage sometimes to reach out to others, but it is critical that we do so. Reaching out to others is the greatest evidence of the Power that lives within us. Joy is doubled when it's divided. It is a great maxim that if you can't find joy, then the best thing to do is to give it away to someone else who is more in need than you are. The joy will then double back to you in ways that you never expected.

ﺨ *From my journal:*
Give your pain and loneliness as a gift to a
friend . . . a gift of understanding.
You never have enough loaves and fishes
until you try and give them away.

T ony Campolo, in his book, *Who Switched the Price Tags?*, talks about the risk-taking necessary to establish friendships.

"During the course of any given school year at Eastern College, I can count on some freshman coming into my office and complaining about loneliness. I can almost predict that the student will say, 'This is supposed to be a Christian college. But if this school is what it's supposed to be, then why am I left so alone? Why isn't anybody paying any attention to me?'

"I don't doubt the loneliness of that student. I am certain that he does suffer from a sense of estrangement. But I also know that the causes of loneliness . . . have nothing to do with the lack of Christianity in the rest of the student body. I know that the student is lonely because he or she is afraid to take the risk of reaching out to others. In the absence of such daring, the paralyzing fear of rejection takes over. . . . But if we do not risk rejection, we are inevitably lonely. Jesus can help us be risk takers. . . . I never tire of telling people that the same Jesus who walked the dusty roads of Palestine 2000 years ago is our resurrected Lord, and He is waiting to be known, loved, and followed here and now."[5]

For I am persuaded, that neither death, nor life, nor angels, nor principalities, nor powers, nor things present, nor things to come, nor height, nor depth, nor any other creature, shall be able to separate us from the love of God, which is in Christ Jesus our Lord. —ROMANS 8:38, 39 (KJV)

ALFRED ADLER, a famous psychologist, once put an ad in the paper for his Fourteen-Day Cure Plan. He claimed that he could cure anyone of any mental or emotional difficulty in just fourteen days if they would do just what he told them to.

One day a woman who was extremely lonely came to see Adler. He told her he could cure her of her loneliness in just fourteen days if she would follow his advice. She was not very enthusiastic, but she still asked, "What do you want me to do?"

Adler replied, "If you will do something for someone else every day for fourteen days, at the end of that time your loneliness will be gone."

She objected profusely, "Why should I do anything for someone else? No one ever does anything for me."

Adler supposedly responded jokingly, "Well, maybe it will take you twenty-one days."[6]

➤ *NTS:*

When was the last time you did something for someone anonymously? The Scriptures remind us to "encourage one another and build each other up" (I Thessalonians 5:11a).

Put a balloon in someone's mailbox, send an anonymous note of encouragement, or send an unsigned telegram that says, "Until further notice—celebrate everything!" Take a tiny step toward enhancing someone else's life, toward helping to heal their loneliness. You might be surprised at how much it heals your own.

AGORAPHOBIA is the fear of being in the midst of open spaces. Therefore persons who have agoraphobia are confined to their own dwelling places by the fear that binds them. It can be emotionally very debilitating and very lonely.

Josie is an agoraphobic and has been trapped in her house for decades. Her loneliness, however, has been appeased by a woman who has phoned her every day for the past twenty-five years. Even when Ruth was in the hospital for knee surgery, she made her daily phone call to Josie. Several years ago, Ruth lost her husband of forty-nine years. By reaching out to Josie, Ruth has appeased her own loneliness as well.

This kind of faithfulness sounded so astonishing, I thought I had better double-check the accuracy of the story. That wasn't hard to do, since Ruth is my mother. And when I asked her about Josie, she lit up with the joy that can only be known through giving. Two people, two lives, two cups of loneliness filled through the act of one person giving without measure to another.

The Book says that it's better to give than to receive. Sometimes, however, that is very difficult. Sometimes people don't deserve your giving. Sometimes people are unresponsive. Give anyway.

People are unreasonable, illogical, and self-centered.
Love them anyway.

If you do good, people will accuse you of selfish motives.
Do good anyway.

Honesty and frankness make you vulnerable.
Be honest anyway.

The biggest people with the biggest ideas can be shot down by the smallest people with the smallest minds.
Think big anyway.

What you spend years building may be destroyed overnight.
Build anyway.

People really need help but may turn against you if you help them.
Help them anyway.

Give the world the best you have and you may get kicked in the teeth.
Give the world the best you've got anyway.

—ANONYMOUS

For if you give, you will get! Your gift will return to you in full and overflowing measure, pressed down, shaken together to make room for more, and running over. Whatever measure you use to give—large or small—will be used to measure what is given back to you. —LUKE 6:38 (TLB)

Breaking the pattern of loneliness requires us to reach outside of ourselves—to God and to others. It begins with a full acceptance of Christ's presence in our lives, a willingness to believe that we are never alone. As God said to Joshua, "As I was with Moses, so I will be with you; I will not leave you nor forsake you. Do not be terrified; do not be discouraged, for the Lord your God will be with you wherever you go" (Joshua 1:5b, 9).

A Guide for the Journey

I never found a companion that was as
companionable as solitude.
—HENRY DAVID THOREAU

æ *FROM MY JOURNAL:*
We cannot overcome loneliness by trying
to escape it. We must lean into it, and
thereby transform it into solitude. We
must not just keep trying to avoid the
loneliness by constant distraction. He is
here. He is here. He is here. We must push
through the loneliness to joy.

RECENTLY I SPENT SOME TIME in the mountains of
West Virginia. The rolling peaks of the Appalachians are so
different from the rugged Sierra Nevadas. I walked along a

pathway which cut a swath through high grass and hay bales. On the ridge were silhouetted trees, leafless, waiting for spring.

Somehow when we see trees like this, we think they are dead; the truth is that they have just pulled their life inward, condensed it in an appropriate economy. All of its energies are pulled into a solitary life within to a deeper core. It is a restrained strength. Less expressive, but no less beautiful. Although they stand in crowded wooded areas, each is alone. Each must find its own light. Each must put down its own roots. Some are bent with pain; some stand eloquent against the sunset. All share that miracle called life.

I saw a deer pause in the pathway. I waited and watched her delicate, hesitant movements. When she finally crossed the path, I noticed another head pop out of the pathway—her fawn. Then another doe appeared with her fawn, and then yet another pair, six in all. When they saw me, they bounded effortlessly and gracefully through the high grass, disappearing and springing up into the air again. When they got to the fence, the first five jumped over gracefully, but one fawn remained behind, hesitant, afraid. Then it found a better place to cross and was gone.

That's how I feel with some of the fences in my life, I thought. I'm not sure if I can get over them, so I wander back and forth looking for a lower place.

I am absolutely alone out here. There isn't another human

being for miles, yet I do not feel lonely. Out here there is a greater sense of God's presence. It's almost tangible. Perhaps it is because there is less to distract me from His promises.

I think my own psalm: Let all things praise Him. Let the hills praise Him. Let the birds praise Him and the grass praise Him and the deer praise Him. Praise the name of the Lord.

I have been lost on more than one occasion in the wilderness. In that situation, given the choice between someone who says, "I'll tell you the way," versus someone who says, "I will go with you," I would always choose the latter. It's always best to travel with someone who knows the way.

Jesus was called The Way, not the destination. It's a journey . . . one step at a time. And it is obvious that a journey includes detours. And there's still the possibility of getting lost.

Sometimes I simply freeze my thoughts and ideas because I'm afraid to make a mistake. I have to be reminded that if you don't get lost once in a while, you're not really exploring. If you're not making mistakes, you are simply not risking enough.

Survival experts disagree on many things, but there is one thing that they are all in concert about: When you're lost, the most important thing to do is to stop. Sit down. Be still. When you are lost, don't just wander.

On one of our Adventure in Fathering courses, Robert, age

six, wandered off to the edge of the forest. He quickly realized that he didn't know where he was. He had been told a number of times by his instructors that if he got lost he should just sit down. After not too long a time, his grateful father found him sitting on a log, waiting.

Robert looked up at his dad and said, "Oh, Dad, I wasn't worried, because I knew if I was lost you would come looking for me."

In Luke 15, Jesus relates two parables, one about a lost sheep and one about a lost coin. About the sheep, He said, "If the one were lost, wouldn't the shepherd leave the ninety-nine in the open and go after the one until he finds it?" And likewise with the coin. "If a woman had ten silver coins and lost one, wouldn't she take a lamp and sweep the house from top to bottom until she finds it?" Both parables insist that we have a Father who seeks us when we are lost.

When we get lost on the inside, most of us start to panic. We wander from relationship to relationship, from activity to activity, from distraction to distraction in an attempt to find our way. Perhaps what we need to do is just sit down.

There is an acronym in survival literature that says STOP. Stop, Think, Observe, Prepare. Perhaps when we get lost on the inside, we need to use the acronym for a slightly different slogan: Surrender, Trust, Obey, Pray.

God will find us, if we wait. Like the little boy who was lost in the woods, we can say, "Abba, I wasn't afraid, because I knew You would be looking for me."

🕊 *FROM MY JOURNAL:*
The feeling of really being lost, of having really lost all your bearings, is frightening. You feel alone, forsaken, and anxious.

Lately it seems that I have felt the gray emptiness of the inner lining of loneliness. No one is immune. I don't care how long you have been a Christian. How mature you are. How many people you have led to the Lord. Loneliness is simply part of the human predicament. It comes with love's territory. When you are truly lonely, simple cosmetics don't work. You can't pretend that you're okay.

Let God really love you. It has something to do with going behind the words to the music. Experience God. Make real contact. Let your heart be thrashed and rearranged. Don't just tidy up. Let go.

Light the fire. Bomb the blockades to your heart.

The most dangerous journey is the journey inward. Jesus bled real blood for each of us—we've got to at least raise our pulse in return.

IN 1975 I WAS TREKKING the High Sierras with Jack Meyer, a lifetime friend. We shared the incredible impact of Scripture on our lives and marveled at its depth—how you could keep coming back again and again to Scripture you thought you knew and understood, and be stunned and refreshed by it in ways you never experienced before.

We talked about how Scripture was meant to be experienced and lived out, not just memorized. It has to sink down into the marrow of your bones and become a part of your everyday life.

For reasons I can't fully explain, I made that day a fifty-year commitment—fifty years—to begin to understand one passage in the Bible, a piece less than twenty lines long that has been used by God to shape lives for centuries: the Twenty-third Psalm. Kids memorize it; people on their deathbeds quote from it; plaques frame it; yellow markers highlight it.

I talk about it in almost every book I write because it describes the essence of my journey and my goal. It is my hope and my inspiration. It offers me peace and direction. It provides a rhythm for my life and a fabric of meaning.

I've read it in virtually every version and in some foreign languages. I've experienced it thousands of times, and it has never failed to excite me, revive me, refresh me, restore me.

I've read it on lonely nights, and it has reminded me of a forever friend and brought me back into His presence. I've read it on nights when my heart was so full of praise that I could hardly speak. It gave me the words I needed. It has been a candle in the darkness, a light of hope. It has been a hiding place and a traveling companion. My Bible almost turns there by itself, but the words are forever new.

Two men were once asked by a pastor to read the Twenty-third Psalm on some special day of observance. The first man was an orator, a man gifted by God with a voice like an angel. He stood and began to read. Each line was carefully metered out, the rhythm precisely paced. Each word was enunciated with eloquence. He moved down through the first stanza and people listened with awe. No one had ever heard this famous passage read with such elegance. When he finished, the congregation murmured their approval. He was good. In fact, very good.

The second man was older. His clothes were not as expensive, and in fact, they needed pressing. He was not nearly as impressive to look at or to listen to. He had to adjust his glasses, and he didn't stand up straight. As he started, he stammered. He had to start again. He didn't have the same inflection as the first man, and he hadn't ever learned how to project his voice. In fact, he was so hard to hear that everyone almost had to hold their breath and listen with more than their ears.

He read more slowly than the first man and, to be quite honest, he had never heard of meter and rhythm. On some words he almost slowed to a stop, as if to savor their fullness of meaning. There were unmeasured pauses, and then very deliberately he would begin again, emphasizing certain words with a power that was not his own.

When he finished, there was a stunned silence—and then the people stood and responded to his reading with a two-minute standing ovation.

On the way out of church, a young man inquired of his friend how that could have happened. "The first man was by far more eloquent."

"Yes, that's true," said his companion. "The first man was indeed more polished."

"Then why the difference?"

"Well," his friend replied, "the first man knew the Twenty-third Psalm. The second man knew the Shepherd."

Over the past fifteen years, I have read and studied the Twenty-third Psalm in every version I could find—not to get to know the Twenty-third Psalm . . . but to know the Shepherd.

During the last twenty years with Summit, the Twenty-third Psalm has been a constant companion. While writing this book, I sat down late one night and wrote a version I thought would be appropriate for this book. It only describes where I am now. Years from now I may try my hand at this again.

God has guided me through the wilderness and the desert, over ranges, through passes. Even when I felt most alone, I knew He was there.

For this next season of my life, I am being invited and called to explore the inner wilderness—the wilderness of the heart. I am new at this. The territory is uncharted; there aren't any maps. So I will need a Guide.

My Wilderness Guide

The Lord is my wilderness guide
  Therefore I am prepared for anything.
In the high meadows
  He invites me to rest.
He leads me beside a river of stillness
  and there He reignites my soul.
He joyfully guides me into paths of obedience
  for His name's sake.
Even though I pass through a valley of darkness
  I fear nothing,
Because I am in Your presence.
  Your rod and staff give me strength.
You prepare a banquet for me
  Even amidst my emptiness.
You anoint my head with gladness.
  My heart overflows.
Your presence and mercy constantly preserve
  me every day of my life.
I now know that my home is where my heart
  is—with You, now and each day for eternity.

The Gift of Solitude

*Draw near to God and He will draw near
to you.* —JAMES 4:8a (NASB)

*To live a spiritual life, we must first find
the courage to enter into the desert of
loneliness and to change it by gentle and
persistent efforts into the garden of
solitude.* —HENRI NOUWEN

IT HAS BEEN SAID that the Christian life is not difficult; it
is impossible. I think what that means is that only with the living
Christ within us can we dare to live out the Christian life.

Loneliness is the gift that leads us to solitude—and without
solitude, the Christian life is impossible. Loneliness parches our
lips for the living God, makes us hungry for His presence.

*As the deer pants for streams of water, so
my soul pants for you, O God.*

—Psalm 42:1

SOME PEOPLE THINK that I am so gregarious, such a people person, that if my days are not filled to the brim with people, I am lonely. In truth, there is a part of me that could have been a monk. I think that is one reason that I enjoy writing so much. It is a solitary activity. It offers me the gift of solitude, a special time with God alone.

"He went up on a mountainside by himself to pray. When evening came, he was there alone" (Matthew 14:23b). We all need to pull away from the endless hassles of our culture—fighting for time, fighting for space on the freeway, fighting for status, fighting for peace of mind.

ॐ *FROM MY JOURNAL:*
*Solitude doesn't transform things; it
simply makes us see things that we
couldn't see before. Solitude invites the
inner presence of God. It's about as
obvious and reasonable as daylight. And
as magnificent. I cannot explain it any
further.*

*All man's miseries derive from not being
able to sit quietly in a room alone.*
—BLAISE PASCAL

A FRIEND AND I DROVE into a gas station recently. The attendant, a young man with pimples and dimples and curly brown hair and a shirt that hung out of his pants, noticed the Ichthus (fish) symbol on the back of the car. He bounded up to the car and in a cheery voice said, "Oh, you know Jesus? I know Jesus, too!"

There was something in the way he said it that bothered me. It was so flippant, so shallow. My friend Craig and I tried to say something about the fact that knowing Jesus was an infinitely deep process, but our words seemed to catch in our throats. Instead, we smiled weakly and said, "Yes."

But that brief encounter precipitated a long conversation about the depth of our privilege of truly knowing Jesus Christ. In *The Province Beyond the River*, W. Paul Jones, a Protestant theologian, seminary professor, and social activist, writes about his courageous journey . . . three months of solitude in a remote Trappist monastery in the mountains of Colorado. It is a powerful account of self-discovery and transcendence. Having spent his whole life reading, teaching, thinking, and writing "about" God, Jones in his own words admits that he had never really experienced

God. Though he was a professing Christian, he admitted to being a "functional atheist."

In reading his account, I wondered if I, too, am frequently a functional atheist. I am embarrassed by the thought of my prayer life. I am ill at ease sometimes with those who thrive on "God talk." Do I really know what it means to practice the presence of God? Have I really experienced God in the way He wants me to?

What would one conclude, I wonder, about a person who spent his whole life dissecting, analyzing, and advocating love, but who had never himself been in love? Is this the kind of Christian I am? Perhaps it describes all of us who never have time for solitude and prayer. We want friends to do what only God can do. We want friends to fill up that space within us that only God can fill.

Psalm 142 was written in a cave where David was hiding from King Saul. Alone, desperately lonely, frightened and ill at ease, he pours out his troubles to God.

> *I cry aloud to the Lord;*
> *I lift up my voice to the Lord for mercy.*
> *I pour out my complaint before him;*
> *before him I tell my trouble.*
> *When my spirit grows faint within me,*
> *it is you who know my way.*
> *In the path where I walk*

men have hidden a snare for me.
Look to my right and see;
   no one is concerned for me.
I have no refuge;
   no one cares for my life.

—PSALM 142:1-4

Dave Roper points out in *The Strength of a Man* that God gave David no earthly friends at this time. He simply gave him Himself. David was alone, in trouble again. In the midst of another desert experience. He desperately needed a friend, but instead God gave him Himself.

I cry to you, O Lord;
   I say, "You are my refuge,
     my portion in the land of the living."
Listen to my cry,
   for I am in desperate need;
rescue me from those who pursue me,
   for they are too strong for me.
Set me free from my prison,
   that I may praise your name.
Then the righteous will gather about me
   because of your goodness to me.

—PSALM 142:5-7

David found that God was the friend he had been wanting all along, because God gave him a new sense of security. In God he was free to "be" a friend rather than want one.

> *Without solitude it is virtually impossible*
> *to live the Christian life.*

> *And if you leave God's paths and go astray,*
> *you will hear a Voice behind you say, "No,*
> *this is the way; walk here."*
> —ISAIAH 30:21 (TLB)

THE CAMEL IS ONE of God's funniest-looking creatures. Its peculiar shape makes it look imperfect and burlesque. It has long, spindly legs upon which there are too-long feet and toes with no shoes. Its long neck holds a head that is too big and a nose that droops.

But the thing that stands out most in the camel's odd poetry of being is the hump—the big, dumb, ugly hump—which is essential for its desert existence. For this is where the camel stores water—an internal oasis. In the desert, where more beautiful and streamlined beasts die quickly of thirst, the camel is designed for survival.

When we, like camels, develop our inner resources sufficiently, we can cross every wasteland and survive arid times without relying on the external. Moreover, it is our hump—that which we consider ordinary and even homely about ourselves—not our beauty, that holds the secret to our survival. Those times of silence, those years of prayer on camel knees, that inner simplicity that we may consider inelegant—these will eventually be our oases in our loneliness, our secret wells of joy.

Aesthetics won't get us across the desert. An internal reservoir of solitude and prayer will. And God's joyful surprise is that our inner resources are what will count in the long run.

&- *FROM MY JOURNAL:*
To be connected with the spiritual means
simply to have a life that flows with the
presence of the extraordinary.

Leslie Weatherhead tells the story of an old Scot who was ill. When his minister came to call, he noticed a chair pulled close to the bed and said, "Well, Donald, I see I'm not your first visitor of the day."

The old man looked up, puzzled, then followed his minister's gaze to the chair.

"Ah," he said. "Let me tell you about that chair. Many years ago, I was finding it difficult to pray. One day I shared my problem with my pastor, and he told me not to worry about kneeling or placing myself in some pious posture. Instead he said, 'Just sit down, put a chair opposite you, and imagine Jesus sitting in it. Just talk to Him as you would a friend.' " Donald concluded, "That's what I've been doing ever since."

The next day the old man's daughter called their minister to report that her father had died. "I had just gone to lie down for an hour or two, because he seemed to be sleeping comfortably. When I came back, he had passed away." She paused. "He hadn't moved . . . except that his hand was on the empty chair beside his bed."

The minister smiled to himself. "That isn't so strange," he replied. "I understand."[7]

> *Learning to enjoy solitude is like eating an elephant—you just take one bite at a time. I'm finally spending time with someone I've never spent much time with before— and that's me! And you know what? I like me!* —JIM WEAVER

> *Where shall the word be found? Where will the word rebound? Not here, there is not enough silence.* —T. S. ELIOT

Loneliness is feeling alone. Solitude is being alone. Loneliness feels frantic. Solitude is still and focused. Loneliness focuses on external circumstances. Solitude focuses on the inner adventure. Loneliness relies on what others think and say about you. Solitude relies on what God says about you and to you. Loneliness is a reaction. Solitude is reflection. Loneliness focuses on absence and all you don't have. Solitude focuses on presence and all God has given you.

All who have walked with the Lord over a period of years encourage us to spend time in prayer and solitude, but most of us feel like we can't find the time or the place.

The irony is that we are surrounded by moments of solitude, if we would only see them. Brother Lawrence wrote about practicing the presence of God while doing the most mundane human chores. When he washed dishes, he washed dishes to the glory of God. He believed that faith was something to be experienced, not something that we indefinitely prepare to do in a special, spiritual way.

Since the love of God was the end of all his actions, he simply established the habit of conversing with God continually, wherever he was and whatever he was doing. Through that he developed "the habitual sense of God's presence." To him there was no distinction between a time of business and a time of worship. He felt the presence of God whether he was working in his kitchen or worshiping in his church.

In our search for solitude, we have inadvertently overlooked some of the simple opportunities that surround us all. There's no such thing as "perfect" solitude. Frequently when I'm in my car, I empty the seat beside me and make a place for Jesus. Then we carry on a conversation in the moving solitude that we have been given. I'm sure some drivers going past must think I'm crazy, talking to myself, but who cares? (I have a dear friend who is constantly saying to me, "Let them think you're loony!") These moments turn out to be some of the most special times of my day.

> *FROM MY JOURNAL:*
> *The heart has a wisdom that the mind will never know. The wilderness of the heart can lead us to a place far beyond mere facts or knowledge. In this age of increasing complexity, we can learn of a simplicity which comes with renewed focus. In an age that exposes more and more the loneliness of being in a crowd, we can deliberately plant those seeds that grow into a genuine appetite for solitude.*

We need to pull away from other people to explore our feelings and discover again that we are fearfully and wonderfully made, complex for a purpose.

Loneliness is like holding a cup upside down under a faucet that is open full blast. The cup cannot be filled because we are not ready to receive. Solitude is when we turn the cup over to receive, to be filled. No one, not even God Himself, can turn that cup over for us. We alone must make the choice to receive God's grace and inner presence.

➤ *NTS:*

Identify some opportunities for solitude when you can be alone with God. You might find solitude

—commuting to work

—going for a walk

—brushing your teeth

—while washing dishes

—after the kids are down

—taking a shower

Resolve to turn these moments of solitude into opportunities for prayer. To remind yourself of the habit you're trying to form, put a dot on your watch. Every time you see it, let it serve as a reminder to pray. A simple format for such times of prayer is ACTS. First a few moments of Adoration; then Confession from the heart; third, the all-important act of Thanksgiving; finally, Supplication—praying for others.

Take a moment for each. Try to do this at least once every hour today.

LONELINESS IS A GIFT from God. A gift that opens up our heart to yearn for His peace. It is a longing for a deeper experience of His presence.

So much of our prayer life is based on our willingness to simply ask. "Ask, and it shall be given unto you. Seek and you will find. Knock, and the door will be opened." One of the reasons that our prayer life is so ineffective is that we keep seeking substitutes and distractions in other people. Perhaps our prayer life won't really be charged with the energy that God wants to give it until we are hungry enough to seek Him and Him alone.

Mark Link tells a story of a boy watching a holy man praying on the banks of a river. When the holy man completed his prayer, the boy went over and asked him, "Will you teach me to pray?"

The holy man studied the boy's face carefully. Then he gripped the boy's head in his hands and plunged it forcefully into the water. The boy struggled frantically, trying to free himself in order to breathe. Finally, the holy man released his hold.

When the boy was finally able to catch his breath, he gasped, "What did you do that for?"

"Well," said the holy man, "when you long to pray as much as you longed to breathe when your head was underwater—only then will I be able to teach you to pray."[8]

When we want God more than anything—more than success, more than peace, more than health—then we truly know how to pray; then we discover Him in fullness.

FROM MY JOURNAL:
Do what you can
with what you have
where you are now.

Be good. Keep your feet dry, your eyes
open, your heart at peace, and your soul in
the joy of Christ.   —THOMAS MERTON

LONELINESS IS AN ACHE that sometimes feels like it cannot be relieved. It tends to be a time of withdrawal, a time when we become preoccupied with our own emptiness. However, loneliness can also be an unexpected invitation to discover God's love and mercy at a previously unexplored level.

God made us for Himself. We were designed for a relationship with the Father and, believe it or not, loneliness is one of the most powerful ways for us to fully understand and experience that. Sometimes the problem is that we are too full of ourselves—perhaps because we don't truly believe that God is enough, that His reality is sufficient on a daily, practical level. So we pursue our distractions and are on the way to becoming "functional atheists," no longer believing that God can fill our empty hearts.

God has spoken very boldly about His desire to be a presence in our lives. If I want to heal the ache and loneliness in my own life, one of the things I need to do is get away alone with God. The paradoxical "answer" to loneliness is aloneness . . . with God. In the silence God will speak to you most powerfully. Too often His words to us get muffled, lost, or covered by the crowd of many noises both inside and outside of us. We must have a quiet heart in order to hear God's distinctive message to us.

Loneliness is both a dying and a birth, a deep pain and a threshold, a heartache and a thirst. Old emotional patterns no longer suffice; the threshold of pain induces a deeper longing and a new kind and quality of fulfillment.

"I will be with you constantly until I have finished giving you all I am promising" (Genesis 28:15b, TLB).

A critical question is, how much love is enough? We must turn and gaze at the loneliest figure of all hanging on the cross and ask ourselves that question. How much love is enough?

&ae; *FROM MY JOURNAL:*
I am troubled. My emotions are raw. My nerves are jangled. Loneliness is certainly no stranger, but God is enough for me There's still so much that I don't understand. There's still so much I'll never be able to do. The pain will probably last for a lifetime, but God is enough for me. My bills are sometimes more than my income. My difficulties are sometimes more than my answers. My physical condition is certainly less than my ideal, but God is enough for me.

My emotions are usually bigger than the corral to contain them, but God is enough for me. Although there are days when it seems like my go-for-it attitude got up and went . . . although it feels like the pain is winning many of the showdowns . . . all I can do is give as much as I know of

myself to as much as I know of God, and
realize that He is enough for me.

IN THESE PAGES I've tried to convince you . . . and me . . .
that loneliness is not a time of abandonment. It just feels that way.
It's actually a time of encounter at new levels with the only One
who can really heal that empty place in our hearts.

Although I know all too well the terrible ache of loneliness, I
also know that the wilderness is a place of great adventure.

Lean into your loneliness. God is shouting to you. Can you
hear Him calling you by name?

Fear not, for I have redeemed you;
I have called you by name, you are mine.
When you pass through the waters I will be
*   with you;*
and through the rivers, they shall not
*   overwhelm you;*
when you walk through fire you shall not be
*   burned,*
and the flame shall not consume you.
Because you are precious in my eyes,
and honored, and I love you . . .
Fear not, for I am with you.

—Isaiah 43:1b-5 (RSV)